T0362952

PUBLISHED BY BOOM
BOOKS
www.boombooks.biz

ABOUT THIS SERIES

.... But after that, I realised that I knew very little about these parents of mine. They had been born about the start of the Twentieth Century, and they died in 1970 and 1980. For their last 50 years, I was old enough to speak with a bit of sense.

I could have talked to them a lot about their lives. I could have found out about the times they lived in. But I did not. I know almost nothing about them really. Their courtship? Working in the pits? The Lock-out in the Depression? Losing their second child? Being dusted as a miner? The shootings at Rothbury? My uncles killed in the War? Love on the dole? There were hundreds, thousands of questions that I would now like to ask them. But, alas, I can't. It's too late.

Thus, prompted by my guilt, I resolved to write these books. They describe happenings that affected people, real people. The whole series is, to coin a modern phrase, designed to push your buttons, to make you remember and wonder at things forgotten.

The books might just let nostalgia see the light of day, so that oldies and youngies will talk about the past and re-discover a heritage otherwise forgotten. Hopefully, they will spark discussions between generations, and foster the asking and answering of questions that should not remain unanswered.

BORN IN 1942?

WHAT ELSE HAPPENED?

RON WILLIAMS

AUSTRALIAN SOCIAL HISTORY

BOOK FOUR IN A SERIES OF 35
FROM 1939 to 1973

BOOM, BABY, BOOM

BORN IN 1942? WHAT ELSE HAPPENED?

Web: www.boombooks.biz
Email: jen@boombooks.biz

© Ron Williams 2013. This edition 2023

Creator: Williams, Ron, 1934- author.
Title: Born in 1965? : what else happened?
ISBN: 9780645182606.

Cover images courtesy of National Archives of Australia:
M4080, 3540397 Womens Land Army
A1663, 8303258 Soldiers wounded in New Guinea
J2879, 1987570 Post Women during WWII
MP113, 33035070 Volunteer Defence Corps mock battle

CONTENTS

IMPORTANT PEOPLE AND EVENTS

Prime Minister	Ben Chifley
Leader of the Opposition	Arthur Fadden
King of England	George VI
President of America	Harry Truman
Emperor of Japan	Hirohito
Prime Minister of Japan	Hideki Tojo
The Pope	Pius XII
Governor General	Baron Gowrie
Leader of Russians	Joseph Stalin

THE ASHES

1938: Australia and England 1-all tie.

1939 to 1945. Play suspended during WWII.

1946 - 47. Australia 3 - 0.

MELBOURNE CUP

1941	Skipton
1942	Felonius
1943	Dark Felt

ACADEMY AWARDS 1942

Best Actor	Gary Cooper
Best Actress	Joan Fontaine
Best Movie	How Green was my Valley

INTRODUCTION TO THE SERIES

I was five years old when the War started. But even at that early age, I was aware of the dread, and yet excitement, that such an epoch-making event brought to my small coal-mining town. At the start, it was not at all certain that it would affect us at all, but quickly it became obvious that everybody in the nation would become seriously involved in it. The most immediate response I remember was that all the Mums (who still remembered WWI) were worried that their sons and husbands would be taken away and killed. After that, I can remember radio speeches given by Chamberlain, Churchill, Lyons, Menzies, and Curtin telling of hard times ahead, but promising certain victory over our wicked foes.

For a young boy, as the War years went on, reality and fantasy went hand in hand. As I heard of our victories, I day-dreamed of being at the head of our Military forces, throwing grenades and leading bayonet charges. I sank dozens of battleships from my submarine that was always under attack. And I lost count of the squadrons of Messerschmitts that I sent spiralling from the sky. Needless to say, I was awarded a lot of medals and, as I got a bit older, earned the plaudits of quite a few pretty girls.

But, mixed in with all this romance, were some more analytical thoughts. Every day, once the battles got going, I would go to the newspapers' maps of where the battlelines currently were. One for the Western front, one in North Africa, and a third in Russia. Later, another in the Pacific. Then I would examine them minutely to see just how far we had moved, backwards or forward. I read all the reports, true and false, and gloated when it was said we were winning, and shrank away at our losses.

At the personal level, I remember the excitement of getting up at 4am on a few days when nearby Newcastle was under submarine attack. We went to our underground air-raid shelter that we shared with a neighbour, and listened, and occasionally looked out, for some who-knows-what enemies to appear. It really was a bit scary. I can remember too the brown-outs, and the black-outs, the searchlights, the tank-traps, the clackers that were given to wardens to warn of gas attacks, and the gasmasks that 20 town-wardens (only) carried, presumably to save a town of 2,000 people when needed. Then there was the rationing, the shortages of everything, and even the very short shirt tails that a perceptive Government decreed were necessary to win the War.

At the start of researching this book, everything started to come back to me. Things such as those above, and locations like Dunkirk, Tobruk, El Alamain, Stalingrad, and Normandy. Really, at this stage these names kept popping up, but I was at loss as to how significant they were. Also, names of people. Hitler and Mussolini I knew were baddies. But how bad? Chamberlain was always criticised for his appeasement, but what were his alternatives? Who were Ribbentrop and Molotov, and Tojo and Blamey, and what was Vichy France?

And finally, when war did come, and grind on, year after year, what effect did it have back here in Australia?. How did we as a society cope with a world that just had to continue on, given that the sons and dads of the nation were actually being killed daily overseas? When the postman did his normal delivery and brought a letter saying your loved one is dead? What did we do when old jobs suddenly disappeared, and new ones were created a hundred miles away? When goods, long readily available, were no longer for sale? When everything changed?

It was all a hotch-potch to me when I started this series. At the end of it, I can say it is a lot clearer. I have sorted out the countable things like battles, locations, people, and rules and regulations. I can appreciate, too, the effects on society, though these can only be ascertained from what I have researched, and make no allowance for all that I have missed.

In presenting this book, I have started every chapter with a look at the military events in the world, first the Pacific, then Europe and the Middle East. Then I come back to Oz to see how we are faring in a military sense within the nation. After that, I blunder about reporting and speculating on which aspects of life here were affected by these, and other ongoing matters.

So, despite all the talk about the War above, and despite the fact that it was the controlling influence on all of our lives, **the thrust of these books is about the social changes and reactions that took place in this period, here in Oz.**

AUSTRALIA'S LEGACY FROM 1941

In the Pacific. Right now, at the start of 1942, Japan was at war with America and Britain. She had launched a sudden aerial attack on the American Pacific fleet at Pearl Harbour only one month ago, and her conquering armies were speeding through British-held Malaya towards Singapore with very little opposition. Both the US and Britain were, for the moment, just now realising that the war that they had been talking about for a year had actually arrived, and were starting to mobilise their military forces to counter the Japanese threat.

The Japanese, though, had not done things by halves. At the same time as they attacked Pearl Harbour, they also launched invasions of many of the nations and Islands in the Pacific. And within a month, just about **every** country was under attack, or had already fallen to the might of the Japanese military.

Note that **China** had been at war since 1937, and that remote (British) Burma would also soon be drawn into the fray, and that later even India would become a potential target. The scope of the Japanese military thrusts was breathtaking in its daring, and quite masterful in its execution. And, apart from that, it was successful, way beyond the dreams of the Japanese, in conquering territories at a speed that the world found hard to believe.

In later Chapters, I will come back to more details of specific places, and campaigns. I just want to now set the scene as Australians saw it at the start of 1942. This nation was under attack from military forces that were vastly superior to our own. The invaders were advancing with frightening speed, and the direction they were moving was towards Australia. Could we stop them if they did come? Would the Brits and the US stop them? Would they even try? These were the questions that were on everyone's lips. And it is these, and similar matters, that this book will be delving into.

EUROPE AND THE MIDDLE EAST

Much of Europe was under German occupation. There were a few neutral nations, like Spain and Sweden. Some nations, like Austria and Czechoslovakia, were German allies. Other countries, like Norway and Poland had been conquered. France, initially an active ally of England in their joint stance against Hitler, had capitulated, and was now a half-hearted colleague of Germany. Her colonies on the North of Africa were in the same boat. Italy had been good mates with Germany all along, and had its troops causing mischief all over the Mediterranean region.

Russia, however, was bent on destroying Germany. The Germans had attacked her half-way through 1941, and after amazing early results, were being slowly driven back. But the battles being fought were huge, and no one could predict who would win out in the long run.

Britain, on the other hand, was very happy, by this stage, to say she had not capitulated to the Germans, and there was now very little chance that she would do so. She had survived the aerial Battle of Britain a year ago, and her land forces were deployed in Middle Eastern and North African lands. And now, with the Japanese attacks in the Pacific, she was mustering a small proportion of her forces for action there. Her main concern was for losses of her shipping, which was being systematically sent to the bottom by Hitler's submarines.

Overall, though, Britain was a lot happier than she had been a year ago. She was still on a full war-footing, her planes were increasingly pounding German cities with high explosives, and she was consistently losing sailors and airmen to German attacks. But she was safe from invasion and, so long as Russia continued to deplete Hitler's forces on the Eastern Front, she was as relieved as could be.

Battles in the Middle East and North Africa were being fought because these places were avenues to the Suez Canal and to the oil fields in the nearby region. Loss of these would have dealt a severe blow to Britain's economy so that, even if they were a long way from home, the Brits were prepared to wage war to protect those interests.

In this book, events outside the Pacific will be covered only if they affect the Australian military, political or social scene. For example, the decisions of Churchill about the deployment of British troops in the Pacific will affect us, and will be covered. But in North Africa, the depredations of Rommel, spectacular though they may be, are remote from our Oz interests, and will at best get brief mention.

AUSTRALIA'S DOMESTIC SCENE

The reaction within Australia to all the recent happenings was one of disbelief. Of course, the war in the Pacific had not developed over-night. There had been plenty of evidence that a crisis was looming, and that the Japanese would soon resort to violence. But in Australia no one thought for a moment that things would come to war. We were not enemies with anyone. Why would we get into a war? But if we did, Britain would send troops and ships, and it would be all over in no time. Then we could also rely on America to help out. And further, the Japanese were a primitive race, their navy was laughable, and their army hopelessly trained. No, said the Australian, there was no chance of a war affecting this nation.

But **in one month**, every bit of this had changed. All our fantasies had been revealed as such. Here we were, possibly all alone, waiting to see if the might of a resurgent Japan would fall on this country. Could you believe it? What had really happened? What could we do about it?

NATIONAL GOVERNMENT

John Curtin was the Leader of the Labour Party, and that Party was in power in the Australian Parliament. The Opposition was made up of two Parties. The first of these, the United Party, was dominant in an anti-Labour coalition, and was run by Robert Menzies. The second was the Country Party, and this followed Arthur Fadden.

The main point at issue here was that Curtin was strongly opposed to forming a "**National Government**", which meant in effect that all Parties should forget their Party differences for the duration of the War, and that they should all pull together. The two Opposition leaders, on the other hand, both warmly supported such a union.

I point out that there are very good arguments for both points of view, and that it is **a matter that we will return to**. For the moment I suggest you note the sense of urgency that pervaded the Letter below in its appeal for what was considered a better system.

Letters, F Menadue. Surely Australia will resound with approval at Mr Fadden's wise speech on unity and National Government. We have been inspired by most of Mr. Curtin's speeches as Prime Minister;

we have admired the resolution and determination of the existing Government; but we have been greatly perplexed that it regards as essential that it must have an "Opposition" – an Opposition composed of about fifty per cent of the members of Parliament.

If attacks were made on our vital shipping, if Darwin, Sydney, or Newcastle were raided or invaded – all terrible possibilities – would this Government still contend it must have a big Opposition to keep it "up to its job," to provide "perspective," etc? It is hard even to treat the question seriously. In these days we all come under one controlling fact, viz, if one goes down, the whole goes down. Any selfish grasping assertion by one class or another would redound to Australia's eternal disgrace and dishonour, assuming she survived such wicked strife and disunity.

Does not this send out a clarion-like cry for a National Government, so that when its leader issues a statement affecting Australia's position in the war and her relations with Great Britain, the United States, and other allies, his voice will be that of the nation, and not that of a party?

His voice will then give utterance to statements expressive of the deliberate judgment of a government representative of all parties and, therefore, reasonably representative of the nation. That Mr Curtin's views have met with such instant and widespread disapproval unmistakably shows that they do not correctly interpret the mind of the nation. A National Government alone is an effective guard against such an incident.

ALUMINIUM COLLECTION

Aluminium was needed for the manufacture of airplanes, and it was in short supply. The Federal Government was urging all citizens, especially householders, to scavenge round and gather as much aluminium as they could for the War Effort.

Letters, A Culyer. May I make a suggestion re the collection of aluminium and other waste? Have a collecting base wherever crowds pass, say, one each at Circular Quay, at Central and Wynyard stations, at King's Cross, Newtown, North Sydney, etc, also one in every country town. Let the people bring their own waste, instead of vans going to collect it.

Letters, E Donnelly. Your correspondent, Mr Phillip Moses, suggests that the Government compel citizens to hand over all aluminium in their possession. Some time ago we gathered all the aluminium about our house and advised the Salvage Department to call and collect it. After waiting months for a man to call, we rang again. In the end the aluminium was relegated to the garbage. One wonders just how badly it was needed.

Letters, One Who Will Give. Women could organise themselves into "aluminium committees" with the approval of local governing bodies, and begin the work at once of house-to-house collections, keeping lists of donors and articles given. One utensil, at least, from each household would be a very slight sacrifice, and in the aggregate would be a substantial help in dealing with the enemy.

ARMS FOR THE PUBLIC

Letters, W Woolnough. May I ask whether the time has not arrived when, in the interests of national safety, it is not justifiable that the revolvers and other arms confiscated from the public a few years ago should be returned or replaced, so as to give every man a chance to play his part in the defence of his home and his womenfolk in the event of an enemy attack? I had to give up, without compensation, a good revolver which I had owned for many years, and which I could use more or less effectively in an emergency.

I suppose all the old Martini-Henry rifles we used to use for target shooting have been destroyed. If not, they could be employed in emergency. What became of all the Italian small-arms captured in Libya and Abyssinia? They would not be suitable for our soldiers in the front line, because of ammunition differences, but if civilians could fire twenty rounds each from such miscellaneous weapons they would assist in dealing with parachute troops and the like. Some of us were good shots 40 or 50 years ago, and could still do some execution with fire-arms, but can do nothing of value armed only with the garden hoe.

Comment. You can see here that the desire to help out the nation was coupled with a quaint notion of what modern warfare was all about. The small rifles he talked about were completely hopeless against bombing from aircraft, and fast tanks, and general blitzkrieg tactics. If a sniper did start to harass ground troops, heavy artillery would pound the area, or flame throwers would attack him, or tanks would make a quick detour to snuff him out. At this stage, well-wishing tacticians were out, and mass murderers were in.

THE DROUGHT

The Sydney region was suffering from a drought. There was nothing unusual about this particular drought, but these were bellicose times, and some people were losing their perspective. The Sydney Water Board had just brought down the severest restrictions it had ever passed. For example, they prohibited hot baths, and they restricted the use of showers except for between 6 and 10am, and 4 to 8pm. Toilet flushing was allowed at all times. It went on to wonder if restricting water supply to a single tap per household would help. Inevitably at the time, thinking about this local drought got mixed up with matters of national defence.

Letters, Alleyne Zander. I should like to know if the vast supplies of harbour water will be drawn on in case of such fires as the one now raging in Manilla being started in Sydney. That this is possible is shown by the example of Le Havre, where, owing to the bursting of the water mains, the fire brigades were powerless to deal with 57 fires. These were ultimately put out with water pumped from the sea.

Letters, K N. Nothing would demonstrate more effectively the incompetence of the Water Board, as now constituted, than the threatened passing of "one tap" regulations just at the time when Sydney is threatened with sporadic fires, and perhaps major conflagrations, in congested areas, owing to enemy action. The householder will have to deal with his troubles as best he can, without any probability of help from the Fire Brigade; and the suggestion that one tap will provide him with enough water for the purpose would be ludicrous if it were not so tragic.

Letters, George Herbert. "Clergyman" is quite right about the urgency of adequate and independent water supply in every home and business place; for the water used on air raid fires would deplete the supply in any mains which escape the bombs.

Why wait for the Water Board to pay for tanks? Surely that maligned body has enough to do? Let those who have waited too long to get iron tanks now roll up their sleeves and dig. A good cement-lined hole, with roof downpipes drained thereto will make a serviceable tank, ready for the next shower and available for fire or thirst.

Letters, Mavis Dowling. Why does not the Water Board assist its ratepayers to install tanks?" Surely the board is not so lacking in finance that it cannot afford to do this, instead of wasting valuable time in warnings and entreaties to the public regarding the saving of water. As "Clergyman" states, the storms which so frequently follow summer days would fill the tanks of every householder, and thus preserve the supply from the catchment area for more vital needs.

The time for words is past. These must now be put into action, and it is surely up to the Water Board to assist its ratepayers in this most serious predicament.

Comment. You can see how the thinking of Oz society was dominated by thoughts of war. In fact, of the 18 Letters published in the *SMH* on the first two days of January, all 18 had some reference to war issues. Given the worsening situation, there seemed little chance that this pattern would change for quite a while.

PROPAGANDA

The Government and the Armed Forces and every State and Federal Government Department by now had propaganda centres working flat out to control the flow of information about Australia, supposedly to the enemy. It also hoped to censor news and information to our citizens so that morale would remain high throughout. I will have plenty to say about the propagandists later in the book, but now I need to make one point.

That is, the information I am using for this book is taken from sources that were contemporaneous to the time. That is, I am gathering information as it was seen at the time. There are a million books written years after the war that contain details that would change some of my accounts. But I have not referred to these at all. **I try to paint the picture as it would have been seen at the time and not with the benefits of hindsight.** In some cases, propaganda obscured the truth, and in those cases, I have often gone on the testimony of the hundreds of people I have since talked to about those events. But in general, the view that I present is the one that, I hope, the average citizen of Australia would have seen at the time.

MY RULES IN WRITING

I give you a few Rules that I follow as I write. They will help you understand where I am coming from.

Note. Throughout this book, I rely a lot on reproducing Letters from the newspapers. Whenever I do this, I put the text in a different font, and indent it a little, and make the font somewhat smaller. I do not edit the text at all. The same is true for the News Items at the start of each Chapter. **That is, I do not correct spelling or if the text gets at all garbled, I do not correct it. It's just as it was seen in the Papers.**

Second Note. The material for this book, when it comes from newspapers, is reported as it was seen at the time. If the benefit of hindsight over the years changes things, then I might record that in my Comments. **The info reported thus reflects matters as they were seen in 1942.**

Third Note. Let me also apologise in advance to anyone I might offend. In a work such as this, **it is certain some people will think I got some things wrong. I am sure that I did**, but please remember, all of **this is only my opinion**. And really, **my** opinion does not matter one little bit in the scheme of things. **I hope you will say "silly old bugger", and shrug your shoulders, and read on.**

OFF WE GO

So now we are ready to plunge into 1942 Let's go, and I trust you will have a pleasant trip.

JANUARY NEWS ITEM

Scouts collect aluminium. Tens of thousands of old aluminium pans to be used in the construction of aircraft were collected by boy scouts at the weekend, right round Australia.

Admission by aluminium. Mr Osbourne of Tamworth reported that, at last Saturday's matinee session, their local picture-proprietor set the entry fee as one pot or pan. The proceeds to the War Effort. Over 1,000 pots were collected.

Scrap iron. Mr Cox, from Belmont, said that in view of the urgent need for scrap metals for munitions, there were old water tanks on almost every farm in the nation that should be used. Old railway lines and old cars were also worth the effort, according to many correspondents.

Wire meshing opinion. "We are urged to put wire meshing on the inside of windows to prevent them from shattering and sending glass flying if a bomb hits. All well and good, but try to buy any meshing and all you get is **supplies are frozen, not in stock, or not obtainable.**

State Governments announced that they would soon make **respirators available to the public**. For example, NSW said that one million would be issued to citizens over the next two months. **They never were.**

The NSW Minister for Education, Clive Evatt, has announced that, after long deliberation, school uniforms would not be compulsory for children attending State schools.

The Sydney Metropolitan Medical Officer condemned the beastly habit of coughing, sneezing, and spitting in public, including trams and trains. He appealed to the public to use their handkerchiefs to cover up.

Supplies of rice for **licensed civilians** will be suspended because the natives of the Pacific islands are now **dependent on Australian rice for their existence**.

The Chairman of the Women's Land Army said that **thousands of women** were being used for harvests.

Several popular **weekly magazines will cease publication next week** because of paper shortage**s.**

The various State Railway systems announced that **women would in future be employed as railway porters,** under virtually the same conditions as the men they were replacing.

The spread of venereal disease among servicemen was lamented by the NSW Department of Health. A spokesman said that the **moral standards of** the community had fallen appreciably since the War started....

Many thousands men had been treated at the hospital since the beginning of the War, and many more go untreated for some time. Excellent results were being obtained with the new **sulfonamide drugs for gonorrhe**a, introduced in 1938.

Production of most lollies would cease immediately in order to properly use sugar supplies. No more feasts at the flickers on Saturday afternoon.

THE ADVANCING JAPS

The war was going horribly for Australia. Our troops were fighting in Malaya, and there the Japanese were moving down the peninsula almost without a hitch. Our defence had no planes, and no ships. And no hope - without them. By the end of January, the enemy were at the south of Malaya, and were clearly well equipped to take Singapore.

The Japanese captured control of the Philippines during the month, and attacked more and more islands of the Dutch East Indies, now Indonesia. To the east of New Guinea, at the great harbour of Rabaul, not far away from us, their planes and then their navy had great successes, and occupied the area by mid-month. Then as January closed, Jap planes consistently bombed the northern townships of east New Guinea.

From Australia, it seemed as if nothing would stop these demons from invading this nation. Our defeats in Malaya was most disturbing, but remote. But Japanese presence in Indonesia, New Guinea and Rabaul was positively scary. Rabaul, in particular, meant that the Japs had a naval and air base close to Australia, and could mount all sorts of attacks from there. And the attacks on New Guinea were obviously a softening up for the full scale attack, and probable capture, of that Territory. That was just a stone's throw away. If anyone was inclined to panic, now was the time to do it.

JOHN CURTIN, PRIME MINISTER

Curtin had blotted his copybook in London and Washington in late December by first of all criticizing the Churchill Government for being so slack in its preparations for war in the Pacific. He said - correctly - that our own difficulties in Malaya came because we had no aircraft or navy, and that the left us at the mercy of the Japanese. He elaborated to then criticise Churchill for sending 500 fighter aircraft to Russia at a time when they would have made all the difference in Malaya, and also the fact that **we still had three divisions of our troops in the European war zone when they were needed to defend Australia's shores.**

Churchill took umbrage at this and said, that as boss of all Imperial Forces, **he knew best** how to deploy them, and that the defence of Australia would be done **after** the Germans had been defeated. A Letter-writer had an interesting view of this.

> **Letters, Bob Lee**. Mr Churchill was elected by the people of England. And next election he will seek their approval again. Australians have no votes in the British elections, although our forces have just been smashed in Greece and Crete defending that country.
>
> Mr Churchill thinks now that he will not send much help to Australia, at the moment, and that he wants the war **near his electorate** to be over first. That makes sense. Would not you do the same in his position?

Curtin was well and truly offside with Churchill at the start of January. But he was in no better position with President Roosevelt. Curtin's sin there was that, after his criticism of the Brits, he went on to say that he looked to America for the military salvation of this nation. Now, Churchill and Roosevelt were great mates, and they both saw that as an impudence in assuming, without any consultation, that America would come to our aid. Surely, Britain could and would do so, at her own strategic timing. What right did some politician from a minute country have to speak for the Governments of the two great Allied Powers? Keep your place, young man!

So, for January, Curtin played with a low profile. However, his Ministers and army officials kept up a pretty steady flow of annoying insinuations that rattled the Brits, and that served Curtin's purposes very well. For his own part, he was immediately interested in getting a place for Australia at the British War Cabinet, and separately, the Pacific War Cabinet if the latter got off the ground. In both if these, he was after **executive status** so that he would have some say over the allocation of Oz troops to the various war zones.

EVACUATION OF SCHOOL CHILDREN
Australia had watched with interest and horror for two years while Britain moved many of its children out of the supposed danger areas of the city, into the equally fanciful safety of the countryside. Over there, children had flowed out of the cities, then flowed back, then a smaller proportion had flowed out again, and then possibly back again. To be nice about a well-intentioned scheme, I will simply say there were **a lot of problems in its implementation**.

Here in Australia, despite the evidence of the British difficulties, there were many people in power who by now were sufficiently convinced that the cities would be bombed and occupied, and that they wanted an evacuation plan for Oz. In NSW, for example, the Minister for National Emergency Services, Mr Heffron, announced that many parents had accepted his recent invitation to apply for help that the Federal Government was prepared to give. He announced that the assistance would consist of half-price rail-fares, for children and poorer mothers. But this applied only to families that could arrange with relatives or friends in the country to take the children, and was not at all a general scheme. To get the cheaper fares, applicants had to jump through many administrative hoops, and sell their souls as well. This **hair-brained scheme** was definitely a first attempt, and was a sure sign that decisions were being made in a political panic.

But in any case, the response rate of **enquiries** was only 12 per cent, and as anyone would know, showed that the children and the mothers and fathers did not want to be separated.

The following writer hit a few nails on the head.

Letters, J Gralton. The evacuation of children from the danger zone seems to give evidence of far too much planning and not enough performance. The day after the war began, the London trains were bearing away to safety in the country their ticketed loads of children in charge of their teachers and guardians. With our war on our own doorstep and the thunder of the bombing of Manila almost ringing in our ears, we should be able to repeat that performance. Get the little folks to safety first and then, if we must, have our questionnaires and ticket investigation, let us do those things afterwards. Every night of delay increases the risk.

The job could be well enough done by teachers, wardens, and police arranging and marshalling the children at the city end with their opposite numbers meeting them in the country towns. No volunteers for offers of accommodation need be called for – the occupants of homes and quarters best capable of receiving them **could simply be told how many they were to cater for** until more suitable places could be arranged. Decent Australians will rise to that occasion.

Of course, there will be inconvenience, bungling, and wastage inseparable from a rush job, but the children will be safe, and that is all that counts. Remember Pearl Harbour; remember Manila. The work should be done at once, without any more delving into income statistics.

The Letter above scarcely touched on some of the problems that large scale evacuation entailed, and there were many more not mentioned. The following Letters make a number of suggestions, some of them sensible.

Letters, Thistle Harris. It is not surprising – nor is it evidence of apathy or lack of interest – that so few children were registered for **evacuation at the schools**. The parents are by this time so confused by the misleading and conflicting reports on Government procedure and policy in regard to evacuation, ranging **from** such statements as "Government has plans in hand for the evacuation of 100,000 children to country centres," **to** "He (the Minister for Home Security) did not favour wholesale evacuation of women and children from all metropolitan areas," that it is small wonder that they feel disinclined to commit themselves to some apparently vague and ill-organised scheme.

Before parents can reasonably be expected to co-operate there should be a well-defined plan placed before them. That this is a job requiring expert organisation is recognised, but, in view of Mr. Curtin's statement that "Anybody who fails to perceive the immediate menace which this attack constitutes for Australia must be lost to all reality", it is one which will brook no delay. There seems to me no alternative here (where billeting on anything but a small scale is out of the question) but for the Government **to requisition large country hotels** in areas considered at present reasonably safe and with an adequate water supply, and to use these for accommodation and educational centres for small children, the younger ones accompanied by mothers. If the liquor licences of these hotels were transferred to some sites close at hand, and compensation for losses due to accommodation profits made, the proprietors or owners of such hotels could offer no objection.

For such a scheme to be successful it would be necessary (a) to provide for **at least one year's evacuation** so that parents would be prepared for a long separation; (b) to arrange for some regular news (probably a radio session over a National station would be the simplest and most far-reaching) to be available to parents so that they might be reassured as to their children's safety and comfort.

There has been some suggestion that the evacuation of the women necessary to tend the children would deplete the city of much needed workers. This would probably be unnecessary in a well-organised scheme. If it is admitted that the education of the children should go on even in a time of national emergency, the teachers necessary for this work will not be available for other work, whether they are in the city or the country.

Letters, M R. The attempt at child evacuation registration at the schools seems futile, particularly as no one even in authority, seems to know how, when, or where.

Show grounds, racecourses, halls, and necessary school buildings could be utilised after being thoroughly cleansed, and disinfected. Districts should be chosen in conjunction with military and medical advisers. **Hessian bags filled with straw** should be in readiness as mattresses and buildings where showers and cooking conveniences not yet installed provided with same immediately. Children should supply own blankets and money for food. Food dumps are supposed to be in place already. Transport to be provided by WANS or similar organisations and railways.

Each school should be evacuated complete with staff under supervision of the head, with exception of domestic schools, which would need to be split up into classes and distributed among camps to assist canteen cooks, etc. Everything should be in readiness for when the military authorities say

"Go." I believe that **compulsion** for any evacuation scheme would be neither kind, wise, nor necessary.

Letters, Ronald Macintyre. With some administrative experience in the last war and in this one, I desire to uphold the Lord Mayor's criticism of "the difficulties and perplexities" in the confusion of plans as to the evacuation of children, and probably mothers, from the congested areas of Sydney. I have no wish to indulge in merely condemnatory language. The position is too serious. But it does seem to me, as to the Lord Mayor, that the outcome will be hopeless confusion, and the result disastrous. If there is any single definite scheme nobody seems to know what it is, and the proposal to hand over the baby to local councils at the last moment makes matters worse.

I venture to suggest that the whole business of the evacuation of children from Sydney be put into the hands of one vigorous and capable man, with ample powers of administration and finance, who will gather round him a few expert advisers for consultative purposes. I would say further that this individual should not be a Government official bound with red tape, nor a politician, nor a military officer, but a capable business citizen, not afraid of responsibility, one of youthful maturity who can devote his whole time to the job and is young enough to work 14 hours a day.

Letters, Alderman and Warden, Lane Cove. The Lord Mayor states that it will take months for the councils to complete the census now requested. Surely the Lord Mayor must know that one of the duties of an NES warden is the compilation of a warden's book, which record gives (or should do) all the information that is required. Whatever the position might be in regard to the city of Sydney, I am certain that outside municipalities can quickly have the matter of the census well in hand.

I certainly agree that the question of NES cost may prove a financial burden to many Councils, but I have frequently stressed with my own Council - and my colleagues agree - that the main point is to get the job done, for the enemy is at our very door.

AIR RAID WARDENS

Wardens had turned out to be a big hit in Britain, and our own local ones were patterned on those brave and hardy souls. Our local lads had first been commissioned over a year ago, right round Australia and had been gradually getting into gear since then. The idea was that a local person, often retired from active work, and mainly male, would volunteer his un-paid services to provide information, and first-aid, and help, to his own locals if an air-raid occurred. They were to be jacks-of-all trades, and had also recently acquired **powers to enter premises on some occasions, and even to make a citizen's arrest if necessary**.

Up till now, they were regarded with tolerant amusement by the general citizenry, who thought that there was no chance of air-raids, and so wardens were not necessary. Now, however, their status was much improved, and when they shouted at night, during a black-out "Put out that bloody light" then most people actually put out that bloody light. But their duties were much more extensive than policing

black-outs, and it looked like they might become as valuable
and respected as they were in Britain.

Many of them went on patrol at 8pm, and finished at 6am.
They often wandered or monitored the neighbourhood
at night, in their tin helmets and WARDEN armbands,
carrying their gas-masks, whistles, and wooden clackers to
alert people to gas attacks. The strain on them was starting
to build. The Minister for Emergency Services stirred the
hornets' nest when he pointed out that warden recruits were
hard to get, and castigated the general population for this.
Some normally self-effacing wardens then decided to go
public.

Letters, E Watkins. The time has arrived when
the public and persons in charge of the various
services must recognise that long before the militia,
Garrison Battalion, and the Volunteer Defence
Corps go into action, the personnel of the National
Emergency Service will have been in the front line,
for the bombing of various objectives is a certain
prelude to any attempt to land troops in Australia.
Whoever controls the supply of equipment has
apparently decided that steel helmets and gas
masks so essential to wardens and others engaged
in National Emergency Services, shall be issued
to the fighting Forces before they are issued to
wardens, despite the fact that the wardens will
undoubtedly need them first.

Telephones, which are an essential part of every
warden's post and first-aid centre, can be obtained
if they are paid for in the usual way, thus putting
a tax on a body of men and women who are

prepared to do a dangerous job in a voluntary capacity when the necessity arises. So long as our leaders continue to adopt the attitude that the National Emergency Services are in the same category as any other hobby, which elderly men and women may take up to fill in their spare time and their weekends, and are not the vital section of Australia's defence which will be called upon first, Mr Heffron's diatribes against the people who fail to volunteer for this service must continue.

Letter, Tom Talbot. I resigned after I had battered uselessly against bureaucracy that wanted me to pay to have a phone installed and for every call. Then in my shift of twelve hours, I paid for a small snack and they would not repay me. Finally, I was rostered ten miles from home, and they would not refund my bus fares. Incidentally, I catch the bus at 10pm, and return at 6am, three days a week, and walk all night. Try it some time.

I cannot afford on my pension to pay for all of these.

Letters, Divisional Warden. May I quote my case as a divisional warden? I am writing on specially headed note paper. This has been supplied to us by a friend. We are not provided with one sheet of paper. I am in charge of five sectors, in which, were I to contact each warden personally, I would have to walk about 30 miles or use my private petrol ration. I avoid this to a certain extent, by continuing to pay the rental of my private phone, which, in ordinary circumstances, due to increasing deductions from my fortnightly cheque and increased phone charges, I would have had disconnected long ago. All my 'phone calls for NES purposes also I have to pay.

With regard to postage I have made an arrangement to have absolutely necessary correspondence posted but not at the expense of the NES. In my position, I have to contact absentee landlords concerning building wardens, etc, and this can only be done by letter or telephone. In addition, I am responsible for personnel of approximately 130 wardens, and often due to issue of new regulations, etc, I have to distribute short notices, which may have to reach the wardens before their fortnightly divisional meeting. These notices have to be provided through the generosity of a few friends.

To organise the division, satisfactorily, because of its extent and topographical features, we have had to establish ten wardens' posts, each connected by telephone, the expense of which is paid by the individual wardens at whose addresses the phone is situated.

Thus it will be noted that the expense of building up and maintaining an efficient organisation is being borne by a few public spirited **"mugs"** who can ill afford such expense, for the protection of the many. May I point out that these few, as well as meeting the expense, also do the work entailed.

Before agreeing too heartily with the above writer, we should have regard for the next Letter.

Wardens' new powers. Wardens had recently acquired some new powers that increased their authority, as I emphasised above. Remember, though, that the number of applicants for the warden's position was well below what was required, so that any person offering was hardly screened at all. It is not surprising if not everyone proved suitable. Quite a few people were wary of this.

Letters, C W N. I am somewhat disturbed by the Minister's action in giving further and arbitrary powers and authority to wardens. This, in my opinion, is dangerous. I have met and contacted many of these men, also women. The great majority are people whose one aim is to do a job of real service and value to their country and fellows. Most of them have been carefully chosen, and possess those essential qualifications of mental and moral balance so necessary in any crisis.

There are far too many, however, in positions of control who are totally unfitted to have any authority whatsoever over their fellows. I have worked with, and under, their instructions, and have found them to be of a most bitter, vindictive, and prejudiced nature. Having only a small authority, their actions and manner have been such as to cause resentment and antagonism from good citizens towards NES work. To give such men the powers and authority of our disciplined and efficient police force is a most provocative act.

AIR RAID SHELTERS

Eighteen months ago the various State Governments and also the Feds started agitating for everyone to get an air-raid shelter that they could use as necessary. They said that householders should build a cave-like structure below ground, or fortify their concrete basements. They even provided a metal and wood do-it-yourself kit, almost free, for interested householders.

Also, **small office blocks** had to make below-ground shelters for their staff and customers, and **bigger buildings** had generally to convert their basements. There was talk at times of using the underground railways and tunnels as well. Some people had heeded these urgings, and many more had not.

Suddenly, interest in shelters became a lot more intense, particularly along the coast. Over the last few months, the building of slit trenches in parks and school-yards had become high on the work-lists for local Councils, as many an unwary walker found out. There were in January, 6 miles of trenches already dug in Sydney, and many more on the way.

Mind you, these shelters had their critics. **Firstly**, the writer below was worried about the slit trenches.

Letters, AQUARIUS, Hosking House. Having surveyed the admirable system of the open cut shelters in the various parks of the city, one is led to the conclusion that the plan is based on the supposition that the drought will continue for the duration of the war. The question naturally arises in one's mind how many and what portions of these shelters will be available to the public after heavy rains, which we are all devoutly praying for?

In many instances the nature of the foundations – largely clay and rock – will not absorb water, and in any heavy weather to get substantial benefit from the shelters those seeking protection will have to provide themselves with waders. Either some movable platform to serve as a footing or pumping arrangement should be devised to cope with what may prove nothing less than water-logged morasses. Of course, a roof could be constructed over the shelters – assuming it to be a feasible proposition.

Comment. This Letter brings back memories of slit trenches in my primary school when I was a lad. As AQUARIUS anticipated, the slits were full of water for months, and became a valuable source of fun for broad-jumpers, with a wet backside for those who fell short.

Secondly, there was this unusual suggestion that shocked many readers.

Letters, Frank Bloomfield. If the code for air-raid shelters is to be carried out, the cost will be, according to various estimates, in the vicinity of £5,000,000, and the amount of labour and material involved would be out of all proportion to its value in winning the war or saving Australia. In principle I believe that to foster the **"funk-hole" complex in our citizens** is wrong and contrary to all the best traditions of our race. **Why should so much emphasis be placed on saving our skins?** Modern warfare does not discriminate between soldier and civilian, and in our attitude towards it, neither should we.

Those of us who are prevented by age or other conditions from taking an active part in the defence of Australia can at least be willing to risk our lives so that the shelters which might have saved us could instead become weapons for active defence.

If we are to be subjected chiefly to sporadic raids from sea-borne air-craft **the answer to that is fighter planes and more fighter planes! Not funk holes!** At the worst, the destruction of a few dozen city buildings and the death of a few hundred citizens, only a proportion of which would be saved in any case by air-raid shelters – would not materially affect the course of the war. But fighter planes to the value of £5,000,000 could and would probably affect the issue to the extent of preventing a raid happening at all.

I feel certain that if a vote were to be taken, then many, many people would support my position.

Comment. I feel certain that most people would not have. Certainly those who responded in Letters did not like it. There can be no doubt that in London at least, thousands upon thousands of lives were saved by crowding into shelters. Further, I cannot imagine any parent saying that their children should be left simply to the mercy of the bombers, and then leave them without protection.

FEBRUARY NEWS ITEMS

Masks for driving. The Federal Government gazetted laws which made it compulsory for all motor vehicles to be fitted with masks for headlights for night driving.

A Letter-writer, wrote that in view of the **shortage of tinplate and aluminium** for the manufacture of toothpaste and cosmetic containers, we should adopt the Swiss approach and make the containers from Bakelite and glass.

Fewer wrapped parcels. An order was issued today forbidding the wrapping of parcels which do not require wrapping for protection. This will require shoppers to use bags or baskets.

Less rubber use. The manufacture of many items made from rubber was prohibited today. The list included aprons, balloons, babies' bibs, football bladders, dart boards, bathing costumes, covers for tennis racquets, galoshes, grips for golf clubs, bath mats, tea-pot spouts, sponges, golf tees, window wedges ….

Tomato crop off market. To supply the Armed Forces with canned tomatoes, an Order has been issued providing that all tomatoes being produced in Victoria or the Murrumbidgee must be delivered to canners and food processors only.

Sydney's Royal Easter Show has been cancelled for the duration of the war. So too has the annual City of Sydney Eisteddfod. Public schools in the State will go back two weeks later than normal after the Christmas break "because of the war".

Spectacles. A correspondent advises that in the event of an air raid, spectacle wearers should first of all remove their glasses. His experience in London tells him that it is easy in an air raid to lose them or smash them

A Letter-writer, tells us that **in an air raid we should invoke Almighty God in** the following words. "Spare Thy people, O Lord, and give them Thine heritage to reproach, that the heathen should not rule over them, wherefore they should say where is my God."

Archdeacon Martin at Saint Andrew's Cathedral in Sydney said that **"God allows war because of sin.** The world has rejected God's Son. The only hope for the world is the gospel of Jesus Christ, yet in many places the Gospel has been trodden under the feet of men. Are we living and working as Christians should live and work?"

Opposition to week-end sport was growing. Some people saw it as using too much petrol. Others saw it as diverting people away from the War Effort....

People who argued for continuation of sport maintained that everyone needed a break from the War, and that no one can continue to perform without some recreation. They said that playing sport had always been seen as a good thing for our youth. It still should be so seen.

In most States, a ban has been placed on the building of new houses.

PLIGHT OF ENEMY ALIENS

A large number of aliens had been in Australia for many years. Officially, they were sorted into distinct groups. "Friendly aliens" were, broadly speaking, those persons who came from a nation in Europe that was now fighting on the Allies' side. Poles and Greeks fitted in here. And "enemy aliens" were from countries that were now fighting against us. These persons were from countries such as Austria and Germany.

It was all a bit of a mess. Many Italians, who had been here forty years, and had fought with us in WWI, were now classified as "enemy". But in fact, they were our fuitos and greengrocers, and owned the local milk bar. Then there were families with an Italian Mum, and a Polish Dad. Could one of these be friendly and the other an enemy?

Then there were the French. Half that country was occupied by the Germans, and so was an enemy. The other half, controlled by the Vichy Government, was not officially our enemy, but often behaved as if it was. Were its nationals enemies or friends? It was a great hotch potch, made worse by the fact that so many different government agencies had jurisdiction over all aliens.

In any case, the Oz public, generally supportive of even the enemy aliens, were now being perturbed by extreme patriots who were claiming that enemy aliens were passing off vital military information to the Japanese. Dramatically, there was a great deal of talk about spies, and a Fifth Column operating here. What this information was, of course, we were not told. Nor was there any questioning of the strangeness of **Italian spies** sending messages to the **Japanese** military. So, new Government rules and actions were devised to keep these people in line.

At the very end of January, regulations were issued to prohibit the **movement of enemy aliens from their home police district** without special permission. This meant that to move beyond their local borders, they had to make application at the local police station, and show they had special business or health reasons for going elsewhere.

This move met with a great deal of protest from aliens and citizens alike. Writer after writer criticised the move and, one way or another, said that it was high time to clear up the position. Either the aliens were dangerous to the safety of this country, and should be interned. Or they were loyal and should certainly have the same rights as any other citizen.

But in times of war, public concern had no chance of affecting Government policy, and so the measures stood. In fact, for the enemy aliens, worse was to come. There had been a lot of talk about itinerant Italians, cane-cutters, from Queensland's North, being in radio contact with the Japanese. The response to this was that police and the army in mid–February raided hundreds of houses in the Innisfail and surrounding areas, dragged men from their beds and took them away for questioning. Four hundred of them were detained, and the next day, were packed into a train and sent inland in internment. The only explanation that Government gave was that the men were "firebrands". The communities they came from were then put on 8pm to 5am curfew, for an indefinite period.

The writer below sums up the outrage felt among the migrant population and most ordinary citizens.

Letter, Horrified Observer. Yesterday I witnessed scenes in Australia that were exactly the same as I witnessed in Poland a few years ago. Our menfolk were woken suddenly, and forced out into the street in their pyjamas. They were each asked a few questions, and half of them were released and half of them were put into trucks and taken away, still in their pyjamas. Some of these returned a few hours later.

One hundred men from our community did not come back. Where they went to, we do not know. When they will come back, we do not know. We have not heard a single word from the authorities.

What is the difference between this and what we saw in Poland? There, people were taken away in the middle of the night? There, they did not come back. Were they to be interned? For how long?

We came to this country full of hope and trust. We have settled in, and made many new Australian friends. We had hopes till now that we could buy a business, and raise our children here. What can we do now? We have no idea. We are obviously rejected and suspected, and found guilty, by the Government. It's hopeless.

There were other signs that times were tough for "enemy" alien migrants. Those who were doctors were **now** allowed to practice, but only if they signed up for anywhere **in their own State**. They could not put their shingles out any place they liked as other doctors could. Also, aliens were **now required to register for the Armed Services,** and apparently would be called up. But not in an active capacity, **only in support roles.** Up till now, they had not been allowed to sign up at all, and while this new level of acceptance might have been seen as an advance, most of them saw it **as an insult and as being degrading.** It meant, as one correspondent put it, **they could not be trusted with a gun.**

Correspondence on these issues was prolific, and mainly from non-aliens. **Aliens were deterred,** like the lady above, by fear of reprisals. Most of the writers were quite ashamed of the way we were treating persons whom we had welcomed to our shores. But there was one writer who thought differently.

> **Letters, Francis Clark.** Have not friends of the enemy filtered into democratic countries in the guise of refugees? Indeed, nothing could be more natural and, on arrival, they would naturally broadcast their condemnation of the enemy. Furthermore any campaign against undue restriction of aliens would suit their book admirably. **It is far better that ninety-nine quite innocent aliens should be subjected to proper restraint than that one treacherous rascal should break through the net to work his fell purpose.**
>
> After all are not all Australians being subjected to restrictions of various kinds? Do these aliens really wish to survive in a free land?
>
> However restricted their present security, it must form a pleasing contrast with the evil conditions they have escaped. If they are wise they will come

to realise that these restrictions will help to ensure that future of peace and freedom which they may hope to share.

One writer, however, answered with a clever question.

Letters, C Pilcher, Diocesan Church House. Mr Clark wrote a Letter in which he argues that, even if only one of a hundred refugees was disloyal, the 99 loyal ones should be interned to prevent the one "rascal" from executing his "fell purpose."

There are certainly some disloyal Australians, for there are disloyal people in every country. We should wonder therefore, if Mr Clark would argue that **all Australians** should be interned in order the check the activities of a few "rascals."

Comment. No one can be proud of the way our aliens, particularly the "enemy" ones, were treated at this time. I know there was the real menace of spies sending out information, but there were clearly better ways of sorting out the one in a thousand persons who was prone to do this. Surely, we did not need the drama and theatre of dawn raids and the like. But, that is what we got, and in war-time, you can't expect much else.

AUSTRALIA IN MID-FEBRUARY

At mid-February, the whites of the eyes were showing in many quarters in Australia. Some people were worried about the war situation, some were deeply worried, and a few were scared stiff. Why would they not be? Ten weeks ago, we were at peace in the Pacific, and all the talk about a war was just that - talk. But suddenly war was a reality. Then it became a nightmare as **everything that could not**

happen, happened. The Japs were seen as a funny little race that could not fight their way out of a wet paper bag. But suddenly, they were routing American, British and Oz forces all over the South Pacific. Singapore was a British bastion, a wonderful military base that would somehow guarantee immunity from marauders for the entire Pacific. Right now, it was about to succumb to a handful of these laughable Japanese invaders. The British Navy ruled the high seas, and yet its two major craft here had been sunk in the first few days of the Pacific war, and dozens of others since then. Where was the British Navy? And where was her Air Force, and all the planes that had been talked about? Britain would always come to the defence of Australia, just as we had done for her in two wars. Where was she now that we most needed her?

What about our politicians? Surely, in these tough times, we would have men at the helm who would stand out for their wisdom, and leadership, and courageous selflessness. Surely, the cream would come to the top. Surely they would forget about all politics and work together as one grand team dedicated only to the nation's survival.

Well, in fact, evidence of all these certainties was hard to find. To most observers, our politicians were doing none of these things. If you looked at the political scene, you got the impression of an overworked Prime Minister, and dozens of his Ministers, and various State Premiers, and their Ministers, each and every one of them pushing their own agenda. Would the PM form a National Government, made up of the best Ministers from each Party? No way. Would the various Ministers stop for a minute and try to

co-ordinate their many war announcements, and their multitude of new laws and regulations? No way. **Would anyone, anywhere** tell the public the truth about what was going on in the war zones, and about the prospects for the future? No way.

On this latter point, the information trickling through was censored to the point of inanity. Granted, we were told when the Japanese captured a new nation. Of course, everything was described in terms of the valour of the defenders, and their determination to win next time. All very Jingoist, but what were our losses, what were the strategic implications, what was likely to be next? None of this was ever discussed. The main question that was **never officially** discussed at this time was whether the Japs would reach Australia's shore, and whether we could keep them out and, if they came and routed us, what would life be like after that.

The Department of Information, that had been set up a year earlier, had been found to be inadequate in its job. So now, censorship and propaganda had supposedly been brought under the control of a Canberra agency, and it started to present a nightly programme over the ABC radio. It supposedly kept listeners informed about the real facts of the war. There was a flood of complaints, all of them along the same lines.

I have included three such below. Notice, incidentally, how they also reveal a high level of dissatisfaction with the politicians and their performance.

Letters, An Ordinary Australian. ABC Radio not only angers listeners, but also tends to weaken both the prestige of Parliament and the morale of

the people. The people want to co-operate with
the Government; such demonstrations make
our co-operation difficult. Have these men no
sense of humour to detect the buffoonery of their
petty self-justifications? Apparently not; for one
Minister seriously defends the broadcasting of this
unedifying interchange as "parliamentary news."
The people do not regard it as news.

I do not know whether this national relay can be
"picked up" overseas. God forbid that it should. It
would misrepresent the intelligence and the morale
of our nation before our enemies and make us a
laughing-stock before our allies, upon whom we
have recently sought to make a good impression.

Letters, Disgusted. I was nauseated by the "news"
broadcast at 10.15 from the national capital on
Saturday evening. A better example of one-sided
party mudslinging would be hard to imagine. How
some of the leaders of Government in Australia hope
to obtain complete co-operation from adherents of
all parties by systematic recrimination is beyond
me. One would expect them to be too busy,
anyhow, for such futile activities.

Letters, A Soldier's Father. The scandalous
broadcasting of the wrangling of politicians, while
our soldiers are engaged in a life and death battle
for Singapore, calls for something more than an
ordinary protest. There must have been many
thousands of people who, like myself, felt literally
sick with disgust as we listened to the Canberra
"news." Who is responsible for the national

broadcasting stations being prostituted to such despicable misuse?

The Prime Minister rightly appeals for complete national unity in these dark days, but what is the use of making that appeal if provocative partisan jibes and veiled partisan insinuations are launched from within his own Cabinet? It is surely high time he used whatever disciplinary powers he possesses to put a stop to this sort of thing; and the citizens of Australia have the right to demand that the ABC shall not be utilised to tell the world that our national unity is a hollow sham. We profess to think a lot of the AIF: but the question is, what must the AIF think of us?

To sum up at mid-February. It seemed that most people were bemused by the suddenness of our military collapse, and wondered if we could turn things around. At the same time, they were not at all happy with their politicians, and **their** attitude to the war. And they wanted more, sensible, information that would inform them of what was really happening.

AFTER MID-FEBRUARY

The fall of Singapore. If things were bad before mid-Feb, they got worse after. At that time, all British troops in Singapore and Malaya surrendered, unconditionally. **A total of 130,000 men passed into captivity.** Of these half were Indian, and **18,490 were Australian. Nearly 8,000 of the Australians would die in captivity at Changi.** On top of this, Australia's battle losses were 1,789 killed, and 1,306 wounded.

News of this surrender found its way into Australian homes next morning via **radio short waves** emanating form Tokyo. Every home in Australia had a radio set capable of receiving these broadcasts, and despite the Government's disapproval, many people listened daily. Once they filtered out the pro-Japanese propaganda, they got a realistic, though exaggerated, picture of how the war was going. On this day, the commentator was over the moon, and said over and over that the fall of Singapore marked the end of all British influence in any part of Asia, and that Britain's prestige had suffered a terminal blow. Even Winston Churchill described the fall of Singapore as "the greatest disaster to British arms that our history affords."

The bombing of Darwin. Four days later, Darwin was bombed by 188 Japanese planes. In two attacks that day, 236 people were killed, an American destroyer was sunk, as well as four merchant ships. All Oz planes based in Darwin were destroyed. The Japs came from bases they had captured in Ambon and Kendari, now in Indonesia.

The shock to Australians was enormous. The war was here, actually here. Australians, just like us, were being killed, and their houses destroyed. The planes came from bases just hundreds of miles away, and we could raise no defence. We were as helpless under air attack as our Forces had been in Singapore. The bombers could come back at any time and repeat their savagery, or go somewhere else, maybe hundreds of miles south. As their armies marched relentlessly forward, they would get more bases, and so their planes could fly closer and closer. Was Brisbane safe?

Or Sydney or even Melbourne? It seemed as if no one, nowhere, was safe. War had indeed come to Australia.

GOVERNMENT CONTROL OF ECONOMIC LIFE

The Curtin government had been under heavy attack for not doing enough. However, at this time, it came out and announced new laws and provisions that gave it complete control of the nation's economy. The nation from now on was "**on a full war economy**", and those people, who had been calling for this, had to live with it.

The main features were that **all wages were now frozen at February's level**. **All prices were also frozen. Sales of real estate were prohibited. Sales of shares** were prohibited. All **profits** declared by Companies were limited to 4 per cent.

There was more to come. **Transfer of employees** between jobs was prohibited, without Man-power Office approval. In effect, you could not change jobs unless ordered to do so by the Government. **Absenteeism was prohibited and a crime against the State.** This applied to workers and to bosses. **Strikes and lock-outs were forbidden under all circumstances. Any area of Australia could be proclaimed as under the control of Government.**

The States wanted to get into this act. For example, a week later, NSW gave the NES permission to **take possession of any building and the property in it, and to requisition any motor vehicle.** Other States followed suit.

Comment one. Critics had argued that the Government was not doing enough to get us on a full war footing. Now, at least in the economic sense, these people had nothing to complain about. The new regulations were as tough as any brought down by Britain, **and were guaranteed to stir up strong opposition.** Indeed, **some of them seemed more based** on Labor Party ideology than on a sound economic basis. Perhaps the desire to get at capitalists came too close to the forefront of their thinking.

For example, the ban on selling real estate. People were being forced to move round. All sorts of families **were disrupted by their menfolk living and dying overseas**, and they wanted to sell up and move elsewhere. Right now, there was a fair percentage of **people moving from North Queensland to the South**. They could not sell. Then again, there would always be people anxious to sell **shares** for one reason or another. **These were not speculators but solid citizens in strife**. There was no provision at all to help them.

Comment two. Everyone was affected by these regulations, and to that extent opposed them. Yet it seemed that, in a sense, they were welcomed. **People had resented the fact that the Government was doing nothing.** With these regulations, they saw that it was at least following in the footsteps of London, and was at last doing **something**. Their efforts might not be the wisest or produce optimum results, but we were no longer living in a power vacuum. **Government might, just might, at last be actually governing. Time would tell.**

MARCH NEW ITEMS

Excess drinking: Drunken servicemen on leave were causing city problems. The Feds moved to reduce these by limiting breweries' production by cutting their output by a third....

NSW did its bit by outlawing pints in pubs.

There would be no Anzac Day marches this year. Also, Easter Monday would not be a holiday.

Authorities advised that there was **no need to move all dairy cattle from the coast to inland area**s. It would, however, continue to monitor the situation.

Burning-off on properties and in back-yards was prohibited so as to prevent enemy aircraft navigating by the light of the fires.

Saturday's Rosehill races were cancelled on the last week in March, **because the Army needed the racecourse**. Further Sydney race meetings would depend on discussions with the Army.

The Government wanted to reduce the use of credit, and thereby spending, in the community. It thus **banned the use of Cash Orders and Time Payments for purchases.**

A ban was placed on the manufacture of cosmetics. This obviously affected women, but also men, in that Brilliantine, hair oil and after-shave lotion were included in the ban.

The Army decided that place names should no longer be placed on the addresses of letters to troops. The letters would be sorted on the basis of the known whereabouts of their Battalion.

The manufacture of refrigerators was prohibited.

Retail deliveries were to be severely curtailed or stopped completely. This would free up more men for essential jobs, and reduce the consumption of petrol. Milk would continue to be home delivered, as would bread, though the number of deliverers would probably be reduced.

The Prime Minister, Mr Curtin, said it was **a deadly sin to do bathroom renovations at this time** when there was a shortage of materials and workmen.

A voluntary **National Insurance Scheme for homes and contents and cars was introduced.** Under it, any such property that was destroyed by war action would be insured by the Government. This was set up because private insurers would not accept insurance for war actions. The premiums were payable immediately, but **any compensation would not be payable till after the War....**

Enemy aliens could not join this Scheme.

Restrictions on trading hours for pubs and wine bars were bringing **the wine industry** to its knees, claimed wine producers.

MILITARY NEWS

The war situation was getting progressively worse. During March, the Japanese kept up their occupation of small islands in the South Pacific, and also the Indian Ocean towards India. But, importantly for Australia, not only was Darwin bombed again a number of times, but also Wyndham and Katherine. Katherine is 100 miles inland, and it seemed that the Japanese front was moving oh-so-rapidly closer towards the heart of this nation.

On top of that, enemy landings were made at a number of small towns along the **northern reaches** of New Guinea. The bombings of Port Moresby were happening every second day, and it was obvious that the Japs were preparing for a push over the Ranges towards Port Moresby. Their invasion of Java was all tidied up, and Bali presented no problems. Further west the capital of Burma, Rangoon, fell during the month, and by the end of March, the Japanese forces had advance another 100 miles towards India.

Everywhere we looked all we could see was that they had, so far, suffered no set-backs at all. Of course, our propaganda machine kept pumping out the usual rubbish that few people took any notice of. It always told us about enemy encounters, and that we had lost 50 men and the Japs had lost 500. Our Air Force always seemed to be shooting down inordinate numbers of enemy planes, and successfully bombing their installations and harbours and aerodromes, yet somehow the buggers kept coming. Government Ministers, of all shapes and sizes, and their Departments and minions, echoed these descriptions, but it was all wasted. There was no amount of censorship of news that could keep from the people the frightening fact that the Japanese were close and getting closer every day. The hard truth seemed to be that, without a miracle, nothing could stop an invasion of Australia.

THE JAPS ARE COMING. As the Japanese got closer, more people every day changed from "worried" to "very worried." Suddenly, to some citizens, attacks of various types were **only days away**, and we all needed to be thinking of how we would respond when that happened. Letter-writers sent their panaceas and advice to the Herald. The Letters below were typical of many that showed what they were worried about. But clearly, the writers all thought that the enemy was almost here, if not on our soil, at least able to bomb and strafe us. **Certain matters had to be attended to, right now.**

Letters, A Smith. I understand it is the intention of the authorities to arrange a march of the various Services, including school cadets, through Sydney's streets on March 6 in connection with the Liberty Loan. Is this wise? We have been told that we may expect air raids on our city at any time. We do not know the hour our enemy may strike, and I question the wisdom of exposing our youth and Services and the tens of thousands of people in the street to such a risk. I hope the authorities will give serious thought to this matter.

Letters, J H S. Waiting for our first air raid, women naturally wonder how they will react. Two things each of us should remember. The noise will be terrific and designed to break our morale – every woman who allows it to make her hysterical aids the enemy. Also every individual in a factory, a shop, or a crowded tram has her individual responsibility to help avert panic.

I have never forgotten an incident in London in 1917. During a musical comedy, the audience suddenly heard nearby anti-aircraft guns go into action. One woman jumped up and ran screaming down the aisle. For one minute the actors wavered and there was a feeling of tense uncertainty. Suddenly, laughing lightly, Gertie Millar danced on to the stage singing a number which followed later in the show. Immediately the orchestra followed her lead, the audience pretended not to hear the guns, and sat through the show unharmed.

One woman could have started a theatre panic. One woman had averted it. It is no shame to feel sick inwardly; it is courage to hide it outwardly.

Letters, Warden. A "full dress rehearsal," including an alert, accompanied by at least a 15 minutes "blank" AA barrage, would greatly assist the general public to face the possibility of raids.

To the uninitiated, an AA barrage can be terrifying even without bombs, and if people are "taught" to know the sound and feel of the former, they would welcome their bark and vibration, rather than fear them.

Letters, H Henchman. I hope that something will be done to preserve Sydney's statuary and memorials from air raid damage before it is too late. Admittedly, much of our statuary is not of great merit, but there are several pieces, such as the Archibald fountain, the Shakespeare memorial, the figures outside the Art Gallery, and those inside the Anzac Memorial that are worth taking care of, to say the least.

Letters, R F B. A precaution taken by the London Fire Brigade, before the blitz began, was the laying of six-inch pipes from the Thames to vulnerable portions of the city. A powerful pump ensured a plentiful supply of sea-water for the fire brigades, and this precaution was undoubtedly the means of saving millions of pounds worth of property.

City property owners here would feel a good deal more comfortable if similar precautions were taken here.

SCORCHED EARTH POLICY

A minority of arm-chair generals had been advocating a scorched earth policy for months. Now, mid March, it was gazette as official-policy for the Oz Army.

This meant that, if the enemy landed in Australia and took command of various areas, then the army should destroy certain facilities before the enemy arrived. These included animals, installation works (power stations), aerodromes, roads, railways, mines, reservoirs, and other materials likely to be of use to the enemy. (The Notice also allowed the Army to prohibit persons from leaving or joining an evacuated area).

Some persons saw this as a good way to slow the progress of the enemy. It had recently been used in Russia, and the Dutch East Indies, and indeed, it had been used for centuries of warfare in many locations. The argument for it was that if the Japs got no support from electricity and food, and had no roads or water to rely on, they would have to somehow manage. This would inevitably slow them down, and might extend their lines of supply beyond their capacity.

There were plenty of others who did not like the idea of scorched earth one bit.

Letter, Felecina Osella. If the military do blow up the mines, how are we, the miners and their families, going to earn a living. If the Japs come, we hope to be left alone if we play along, and we will want to survive with the money we will earn in the mines. If they are all blown up, then we will all starve. We will probably then be herded away from our homes and put to work somewhere else to get some production out of us. But, then, if scorched earth has been done everywhere, there will be nowhere for us to go. What happens then?

Letters, I Idriess. With the one exception of the evacuation of mothers and children from threatened areas, let us immediately cease advocating "scorched earth," "mass evacuation of stock," "demolition of towns and works and homes," "smashing motor cars," etc., and general "destruction!" policy. We must remember that too much of this "scorched earth" advocacy tends to make too many anxious people fearful before we start fighting. Scorched earth and destruction savour too much of Malaya and Burma and the unfortunate Dutch East Indies and the too numerous defeats with which, alas, we are by now so sadly familiar.

Give us a rousing war cry and a lead to fight like hell. That's all we want.

Letters, A Elkin, Professor, University of Sydney.
Away with all this talk of "scorched earth" and "evacuation" of any except the aged, infirm and very young! Such is the cry, but why? Not only to rid ourselves of a defeatist and retreating attitude, but because if we have to scorch the earth and evacuate the coast we shall already be defeated. The Russians could retreat hundreds of miles and still live off the earth and continue their industries. But once we scorch our coastal belt and retreat from two hundred to three hundred miles inland, we enter a zone of sparse pastoral country and spasmodic crops – we go to land which is only too frequently scorched by nature.

We are told to be realists. Very well! Could the people and armies of Perth and Fremantle exist in Kalgoorlie, which depends for its water supply on one pipeline 350 miles in length? Could the million and a half population of Sydney, Newcastle, Maitland and Cessnock retire to a line from Canberra to Gilgandra and live? To go further would be suicide. And similarly with other thickly populated areas.

The point is, we either defeat the enemy on the coastal strip or we are defeated. We cannot scorch the earth and go back and live.

Let our slogan therefore be positive. "Australia goes forth to war." It is no longer a matter of sending an expeditionary force to do battle: we must all go forth – the fighting Forces, the factory worker, the miner, the business person, the householder, you and I. At work or off work be always on duty. Geographically we cannot go inland, but we can go forth. Let us then go forth!

LET THEM COME

A Queensland politician successfully objected to the display of posters, supposedly for propaganda, from the Department of Information, which showed a ferocious Japanese soldier overshadowing a map of Australia, and eyeing it with contempt. The people here were cowering and running away. The heading was on the poster was "He's coming South", the idea behind it was to scare Australians, and make them more obedient and ready to work harder.

The *Sydney Morning Herald* also took exception to the craven message being delivered, and said "it is not as an Australia shrinking before this giant shadow that we want to be seen by the world. Nor should we harp on aspects of safety, and correct methods of withdrawal. The right slogan should be '**go north and throw them into the sea.**' That is the robust spirit of Australia. Our propaganda should express and embody it."

Letter writers joined the attack with enthusiasm.

Letters, I McDowell. The propaganda most effective at the present time would be pep-talks such as the football coach uses regarding the "last ounce that wins." Our Allies combine three-quarters of the world's population, 90 per cent of the world's oil, the incomparable mass production and raw material of the United States, the unlimited man-power of China. In addition to this, we have our Navy and Air Force, and the indomitable determination of the British people.

Surely that is a more dynamic force than the clawing hand of fear?

Letters, G Foster, Quarrymen's Union, Sydney. The sooner we get someone in authority who understands the psychological effect of propaganda the better for Australia. The poster "We dare not fail," showing a fearful woman with a child in her arms, is just about the worst type of rubbish which could be foisted on to our national pride in the name of propaganda. The next step will be depicting an AIF hero on his knees, begging the Jap to "don't."

On top of this we read that the Department of Information is "going ahead with the much-discussed 'Fear poster'." Where does all this wonderful originality come from? Australia has the finest fighting material in the world, proven on many bloody fields, and because we have had a few set-backs from the Jap, through no fault of our soldiers, the Department of Information is going to put "pep" into our people by trying to frighten them.

It seems to me that the fear psychology has roosted itself in the Department of Information. If that "fear" poster is flooded through this fair land of ours, the people will be justified by rising in their wrath, and using the famous saying of Jackie Fisher, "Sack the lot."

Letters, C Rawson. The people of Australia must surely feel frustrated and amazed at the defensive and futile propaganda which goes over the air day after day. Surely it could do no harm, for a month or two or more, to change over to aggression and the offensive, and endeavour to swing the nation over to a frame of mind which will enable it to collectively have the will to fight and the will to win. Cut out the fright posters, too, and give us one or two with a Jap on the end of a good Australian bayonet, and the slogan, "If he comes, we'll throw him out."

LET'S BE REALLY OFFENSIVE

Developing these ideas, the *SMH* correctly guessed that now was the right time to suggest to the nation that what we needed was a truly aggressive stance towards the Japanese. It argued that fears had to be displaced by determination, that we should meet force with even more force, and that heroism was an attribute that the common man could rise to.

Its little crusade appeared to bear fruit, at least among its readers. Subsequent Letters all showed a much greater resolve than earlier ones. As the topic died down, the resolve remained but was supplemented a little by moralistic and religious additives.

Letters, Old Soldier, 1ˢᵗ AIF, Lindfield. When is the "offensive spirit" envisaged in recent "Herald" articles and leaders about to begin? With the shining example of brave Dutch allies in the Indies before us, surely every Australian worth his salt is now prepared to go forth and meet the invader – not wait here for him.

Defeatism and retreatism must be dropped and our attitude readjusted for the all-in fight to come – as come it must, soon. Apathy, that soul-destroying and peace-time attribute, must be shed for the obsolete cloak it is. Every citizen should at least join the VDC, ARP, if not the AIF.

I envisage a legion of bushmen formed to outflank and outwit the yellow curse at the same game he has practiced to advantage in the countries he is overrunning. Just imagine a Jap beating our bushmen on their home ground – but be sure it is bushmen who meet him there! Australian soldiers do not hold the Jap in the respect or awe he deserves (while not making the mistake of under-estimation), and can meet him man for man with more than confidence. Australian civilians – embryo "Diggers" all – can go forth to meet him in the same spirit.

Letters, A E M. I was pleased to read your leader in which you advocate a policy of aggression in place of the spirit of fear which pervades the minds of so many at present. Recently I went to the Government insurance office to insure my goods and chattels and was astounded to observe the air of depression and defeatism which seemed to pervade the place. For instance, the clerk who attended to me almost persuaded me that it was hardly worthwhile even insuring my property, as it was a foregone conclusion that we were going to be invaded, and what was the use! Is that the best type of man that the Government could put into a job of that sort?

Letters, Norman Pardey.   There is no doubt about the material forces that shall be hurled against Australia when the time suits the enemy. It is important and imperative that we concern ourselves urgently with the material forces that must meet the cruel and powerful aggressor when it strikes. But are we forgetting that we are fighting for a righteous cause and that the God of all righteousness is using the British Commonwealth of Nations and her Allies as human instruments to promote goodness, truth, and freedom and to set at liberty them that are bound?

We believed in this at the beginning of the war, when the fight was remote from our shores: surely we are not prepared to sell our birthright at Australia's "finest hour." God, the Supreme Spiritual Force, together with those unseen spiritual forces, a mighty host, who down through the ages fought valiantly in the fight during their earthly pilgrimage, and who now not only cheer and beckon us on, give us a peculiar strength and inspiration, as we prepare for the final struggle.

The Christian faith is not something to be talked about, and a subject for religious literature during the days of peace; it is that which gives man an added courage and fires his zeal and supplements his material resources so that, like the leaders of ancient times and those Christian generals who helped to build up this Empire, used spiritual forces and knew that defeat was impossible. The Christian nations are challenged as never before, let us confidently meet the challenge on our own soil, using every force at our disposal, physical and mental, and also those spiritual forces which will supply us with guidance and inspiration and victory.

Letters, Stuart Gurr. Certain people will not grasp essential facts. They live in a world of self-deception, ignoring realism because they have not the courage to face it. So they make a carnival of life – drink, gamble, and debauch in a vain effort to evade issues and dull their own fears. We cannot beat an enemy, trained for conquest over many years, in hotel bars and night clubs. That depraved spirit which dances and **frivols** while the enemy hammers at the gate, will clutter up the roads when the more sturdy, courageous, and patriotic elements move to get to grips with the enemy. An Australia with the pioneer spirit of its forbears, abandoning follies and the pleasant paths of life, roused and trained for action, both men and women, will drive the Japanese hordes back into the sea. But they must wake up, abandon selfishness, and steel themselves for crises.

POST SCRIPT FOR MARCH

In the last week of March, a glimmer of hope appeared. It was just a small glimmer, more the flame of a match seen though a forest. But it was better than the blackness without it.

It came from America. The most obvious sign was the **appearance on the scene of General Douglas McArthur.** He arrived on Australia with a (very exaggerated) stirring story about the risks he had taken to get here, and paraded round the nation like the Supreme Commander that he was.

He said many stirring things at a time when there was a hint of defeatism in the air, and so he was doubtless good for morale.

Importantly, though, **there was more to it than that**. He and his men let it slip out that much men and weaponry had recently been shipped to Australia. Then there were other good signs. The newspapers started reporting in Brisbane that fights had broken out in pubs on the last two Saturday afternoons between Australian and American soldiers. Surely this meant that the Yanks were arriving here in numbers. At the same time, clergymen started arguing among themselves in the Press about whether they would consecrate our girls marrying US soldiers. It turned out that five marriage licences had already been applied for. To top it all, military reports came through that our planes had bombed the Japanese on the northern ports of New Guinea. It seemed that our planes were accompanied by US Super Fortress bombers. **These were the first inklings that the Yanks were coming.** We had no idea of how many, and what they could do, but it seemed that maybe some serious help just might be on the way.

At the very end of the month, more welcome news. A War Council was set up in Washington, with Australia represented. It looked like the operation of the War had been taken **from the hands of Churchill and the British,** and given to the US, with definite input from Australia. It had become clear over two weeks **that McArthur was indeed Supreme**, and that he would prove that by doing things his own way, without much interference or delay from anyone. To Australia at that time, that seemed to be what we wanted. Indeed, to many people it was just the type of leadership we needed. To these people at least, there was a little light on the horizon.

HOME DELIVERIES

Home deliveries of many kinds are to cease by mid-May. These include meat, groceries, fruit, rabbits, and clothes-props. Milk, ice and bread deliveries will continue, but areas will be zoned so that **only one provider can service a single area.**

One objection to this was that what would happen if the one supplier in your area was not satisfactory? Or if he became arrogant and annoyed lots of people in his zone. How could he be disciplined? What if he did not carry a type of bread that you wanted? How could you then shop around if other suppliers were not allowed to sell outside their zone?

The answer to these was there was nothing you could do. Everyone had to make sacrifices, and these were sacrifices shared by everyone in the nation.

APRIL NEWS ITEMS

Rain fell in NSW, and people can now **take hot baths**. To a depth of four inches.

The Trans Continental Train from Port Augusta to Perth was cancelled for the duration of the War.

Railway stations across the nation were made to **remove their names from view**. This was supposedly to prevent the enemy from knowing where they were.

NSW has closed **150 small country schools** because of a shortage of teachers who have enlisted in the military.

The incidence of **crime during brown-outs at night** was worrying authorities. They claimed that the number of petty thefts and assaults had increased because the offenders could get away with it in the dark.

The State Emergency Services is having difficulty maintaining its head count. A number of wardens are leaving after two years, dissatisfied with the way they are treated and the costs they are forced to bear. On the other hand, new recruits are hard to find because of the same reasons.

On Anzac Day, there were no marches, pubs did not open till mid-day (at the earliest), and there was no organised public sport.

The size of the Womens' Army will be increased from 1,000 to 8,000. Women are encouraged to recruit, and they are informed of an immediate need for vehicle drivers.

Racing Clubs will be restricted in the number of race meetings they can hold. All major cities will have to **forego one meeting per month**. Country clubs will lose many meetings, yet to be determined. **Promoters of boxing** proposed that they should run boxing events on Saturday afternoons when **there were no races**. John Curtin said this was not acceptable.

Raffles where clothing is offered as prizes are now prohibited. Persons guilty of such a crime will face up to six months imprisonment and one hundred Pounds fine.

Women teachers in NSW are now allowed to wear **slacks and bare legs to school**.

Diners in restaurants will in future be offered a maximum of **three courses** from a **fixed menu**. Maximum prices will be fixed by law.

Army dodgers were warned today by a number of officials that a blitz on them will be conducted soon. Persons who will be targetted will be those who feign medical problems.

There are **100,000 Australians enrolled as wardens**.

Australia's henceforth would be compelled to have **two beef-less day per week**. That means that persons supplying, selling, or buying beef on those two non-consecutive days would be subject to severe penalties.

The Federal leader of the Opposition, Mr Hughes, said today that the nation would benefit if people **would only smile more**.

THE EUROPEAN SCENE

Britain was still very worried about **submarine attacks**. The shipping routes from North America were under constant threats that were not decreasing. The subs were also turning up off the coast of South America, and out in the Indian Ocean. The fact that American long-range planes were harassing them was having some positive effect, but still they were a long way from beaten.

The RAF was riding pretty high. Day after day, they launched massive attacks on German-held positions, and bombed the living daylights out of them. It was sometimes argued that they had little military effect, but it was quite clear that they were impeding the Nazi war effort. Occasionally, the Germans launched "reprisal" raids on England, and while these were still terrifying and damaging to civilians, they were small relative to eighteen months ago. Britain by now was certain she would not be invaded.

In North Africa, the Brits were holding their own at the moment. Fighting there had swept backwards and forward across Libya for two years, and now forces appeared stuck in the middle. Remember that all this fighting in the desert was **to stop the Germans from invading Egypt**, and getting control of the Suez Canal. While ever the War there was still outside of Egypt, things were not all that bad. So, at this time, the Brits were a bit complacent. But, I happen to know, this situation would not last. Rommel had some aces up his sleeve.

Russia, meanwhile, had been successful in surviving the worst that Hitler could throw at her. In fact, she was now turning the tables on the Nazis and pushing them back towards where they had come from. But they were aware that when the winter thaw was over, and the ground again became passable, **the Germans were intending to counter-attack**, and so their feelings of relief were tempered by caution.

THE OZ MILITARY SCENE

Things got worse in April. The Japanese conquered more islands in the Dutch East Indies (Indonesia), and in particular, took possession of big oil producing regions. The Dutch, as they retreated from these fields, used a scorched earth policy, but really this only inconvenienced the Japanese for a few days. Importantly, the Japs were able to capture a number of areas that would make good air bases for their planes, and this just added to the threat to Australia.

Along the north coast of New Guinea, they were once more successful, and met with no land resistance. And the bombings of Port Moresby and Darwin went on every second day. But, and this was encouraging to all Australian, our air attacks, along with increasing American intervention, were reportedly taking a bigger toll on the bases that the Japs were trying to establish there.

Over in Burma, the position looked hopeless, as the Japanese advanced with almost lightning speed. Ceylon was now apparently a target in the sight of the Japs, and was watching a huge fleet make its way deliberately toward itself.

So, on the surface, the situation only got worse. But internally, Australia felt a bit better. We could see that the

Allies were producing more planes and arms, and that Americans were popping up everywhere, and they were bringing with them all sorts of supplies that we needed. We also felt better about out air raids on northern New Guinea. It seemed that **we were shooting down as many planes as we lost**, and that was ever so much an improvement. **Maybe all was not lost.**

CURTIN AND CHURCHILL

There two gentlemen were at each other's throats again. Curtin had been battling for months now to get Churchill to release three Divisions of Australian Army troops, so that they could come back to Australia. Churchill, on the other hand, said that they were needed in Europe and the Middle East, and that when the War **there** had been won, the entire Empire would send the Japs back home. Curtin's quite sensible demands were met, time and time again, with the argument that Churchill and Washington needed to have a master plan, and that Australia's interference was just that – interference.

At the start of April, Curtin was gradually winning. By then, Churchill had released two of the Divisions, and they were on their way home. Not only that, Washington had appointed McArthur as Supreme Commander of the South West Pacific forces, with Australia's approval, and the aggressive nature of the man made it obvious that it would be **on his say alone that Australian troops would be deployed.** Curtin thought, correctly as it turned out, that this would be much better than control from London where, it was alleged by some of our citizens, our troops were thought of as being more expendable than others.

Curtin also thought, once again correctly to my eyes, that they were our troops and, in this period of dire need, that they should be protecting our shores.

Curtin, however, was not having it all his own way. For example, granted some of our troops were on their way home, but Churchill diverted two Brigades of them to the defence of Ceylon, and they were kept there for four months. This was over the "dead body" of Curtin. Then again, hundreds and hundreds of fighters and bombers were flying from Britain every night to harass European enemy forces. What about, said Curtin, a few hundred of these planes, and pilots (many of whom were Australian), being sent home now? They could be here in a week, and what a difference these experienced pilots, and their fast planes, would make to our defence. But, said Mr Churchill, not on your life.

So, things were only middling between the two leaders. The big effect that all this was having was that Australians en masse were no longer thinking of Britain as a savior, and were turning instead towards America. It's **just as well we did.**

SMALL BOATS GONE FOR THE DURATION

News Item, March 27. NES Regulations were proclaimed Australia-wide. They decreed that **all motor boats, launches and row boats would be handed over to the Navy** and various authorities, and they **would be removed to collective storage place**s. This applied to all boats on the coast, in estuaries and rivers and on lakes. Once the boats were in the storage places, owners would not have access to them until released by proclamation.

The aim was to ensure that no small boats fell into enemy hands, enabling them to launch attacks along the coast and up rivers. Boats in Sydney Harbour would be excluded from this Regulation. Fishing boats, and small ferry operators, would be excluded. Boats from outside the Harbour would not be permitted to re-locate in the Harbour.

Such boats had to have their engines or part thereof removed to incapacitate the boat. Rowlocks and oars must be removed from row boats. Boats already in storage in boatsheds must be brought out and floated in places where the Navy could readily seize them. If a boat could not easily be moved, it would be scuttled by the Navy.

No compensation would be paid for the removal of the boats.

Comment. It is obvious that this was not a popular order. One big objection, repeated over and over by Letter writers, was about the wastage of Navy manpower. Should not the Navy be up in the Dutch East Indies fighting the Japs? A few other complaints are shown below.

Letters, H Sutton. The proclamation requiring the collection of launches and other small craft – not for military use, but to be stored – is not only unjust, but detrimental. We Australians want to defend ourselves, but when the Government makes proclamations to take away from us our right of defence, they show a lamentable misunderstanding of good judgment and strategy. They commandeer our guns, boats, and other means of defence and ask us to defend ourselves. This is childish. Let us act like grown-up men and women.

Wooden craft if left in the water for any length of time would be riddled with borers and other sea pests. On the other hand, if it were intended that the boats should be lifted out of the water and left uncovered it would be no time before the planks opened and the boats became valueless. If it is the Government's intention that these boats be given the necessary care to preserve them, the cost of protection would run into thousands of pounds and all to no purpose.

I am sure that 99.9 per cent of Australians have enough discretion and initiative when danger presents itself; the craft left to the .1 per cent would not carry many Japanese. The scheme should be reviewed. It is an insult to our intelligence and to our integrity.

Letters, R Mason. A fortnight ago a notice appeared calling on all boat-owners immediately to put their boats in the water so they could be collected by the Government, and taken to a place of safety. Most of these boats had been out of the water and stored for months on account of petrol rationing, the result being that they were anything but watertight.

However, I, like hundred of others, thinking the matter urgent and that the boats would be collected in a day or so, immediately complied with the order. Imagine my surprise on going out last weekend to see the boats still there, but under water (as was only to be expected after 14 days), with the engines practically ruined by salt water, and all electrical equipment just a heap of junk.

If it was such an urgent matter as we were led to believe, why have the boats been left so long? And are the owners who complied with the notice (against their own judgment) to receive no recompense whatever, or are we to be penalised? Some of us can ill afford to suffer this loss ourselves – a loss caused by no fault of ours.

STOP PRESS. News item, April 30th.

The Minister for the Navy, Mr Makin, said in the House of Representatives yesterday that, because of floods in the Hawkesbury River area, **165 boats seized by the Government had been destroyed, and 90 others damaged.**

TEA RATIONING

Press Announcement. April 30th. Tea rationing will operate in Australia from today, with an allowance of one ounce a week for each person over nine years of age.

One person in each family is to be responsible for the registration of other members. He will be required to declare to his tea retailer (normal grocer) his name and address; names of persons over age nine for whom he is responsible; the aggregate quantity of tea currently held by him; and that he is not registered elsewhere.

The ration will be available each fortnight in capital cities, and each month elsewhere. Retailers must send completed forms to the Division of Import Procurement in Sydney of

Melbourne. This move is made necessary by the loss of imports from our sources in the Dutch East Indies.

Where a person legitimately changes address, he must notify his old grocer of the change, and also register with his new grocer. The Customs Department said that the rationing scheme would be strictly policed by special officers, and high penalties could be imposed on those who broke the ration law.

It was expected that, depending on the strength of the brew, the ration will provide **one cup per person per day**.

Comment. Remember, tea was a vital drink in Australia at the time. **There was no coff**ee, and tea was the liquid staff of life. People of all ages, accustomed to eight cups of tea a day, really suffered when cut back to one. Requests for alleviations were common, and I publish two such brief pleas below.

Letters, 75, Mosman. Elderly people and invalids need a cup of tea several times a day, and to provide them with this stimulant is more vital than the wharf-labourer's beer. Will the Prime Minister favourably consider stretching the regulation to allow double rations to people over 70 and invalids?

Letters, Soldier's Wife, Roseville. Now that the anomaly of the "tea clubs" is to be investigated, would the Tea Commission, in all fairness, consider the case of soldier's wives, and allow then 1oz of tea per fortnight for a husband's ration? When the boys come on leave, they look forward to a good cup of tea, and if, as many do, they bring home a country soldier with them, the oz per week allowed the wife at present does not suffice.

DEVELOPMENT OF POLICIES

Letters, Oscar Trebitsch. Since the Premier feels uneasy about the insecurity of the darkened streets, I wish to draw attention to the amazing waste of time and energy enforced on the Police of Sydney. Every day in all stations policemen are busy filling in hundreds of "travel permits" for refugee-aliens, because indiscriminately all of them, even wives and old parents of men who are now loyally serving this democracy as soldiers and of the men who volunteered but were medically unfit, must as "enemy aliens" have a permit if they are so daring as to visit their children living in the next district of Sydney.

As the Police are so busy watching the shopping of elderly refugee ladies, there are not enough of them to watch the streets of **Sydney at night.**

Comment. **The Letter** above made the point that the authorities were still enjoying themselves harassing so-called enemy aliens. The Letter **below** follows on, and opened up a subject many people were interested in.

Letters, B Pettit. It is becoming obvious that many of the men and women placed in authority during these War-years are not suitable for their posts. It is not surprising. Most of them were nobodies in their previous jobs, and have no experience of anything. Many of them are now politicians in charge of Departments, and can change the lives of millions of people without any thought of being questioned. If anything goes wrong, they can wrap themselves in the War blanket and say it cannot be discussed for security reasons.

For example, a few months ago, trading on the Stock Exchange was prohibited. That ban lasted **only two weeks**. At the same time, sales of houses were stopped. Again, only **for two weeks**. There are plenty of examples of all sorts that show up government ineptitude on a grand scale.

Recently, for example, **the Navy** was called upon to find and remove thousands and thousands of small boats to new locations. Surely, if this move is necessary – and no one I know thinks it is – it should be done by anyone except the Navy. They should be up north fighting the Japanese. Then again, **the police** are wasting their limited time issuing permits to enemy aliens so they can go shopping. Yet we hear all the time about the increase in crime in the brown-outs. Draw your own conclusion.

It comes down to people who are not competent being given power and abusing it. Surely these people can sit down and think through their policies and take expert considered advice. But they don't. As soon as they get an idea, they rush out and tell the Press about all the good things they are doing, and that whatever it is, it will win the War for us.

We need sober, experienced, deliberate people making our policies. We have only a handful of them now.

Comment. Mr Pettit makes a point that seemed worthy of answer. In War years, though, the powers-that-be rarely answered anything.

SUNDAY ENTERTAINMENT

The streets of the capital cities were full of troops on weekend leave on Sunday evenings. These had grown to a crowd in recent months, and were now swelled by Americans. On Saturdays, many went to pubs and then night clubs, and were off the street. Now, on the dead Sundays in our cities, they simply wandered, and felt lonely and unwanted. Some of them got into trouble.

The Churches generally were strongly against opening up entertainment venues for these waifs. Their arguments were based on their idea of the sanctity of Sundays, and the fear that "European Sundays" would come to Australia. Some of their opponents were entrepreneurs who knew there was a profit in homeless troops. Others were more genuine and said that troops had every right to do what they wanted, and that the "wowsers" should stay at home, but let others get some sort of fun out of life.

After much argument, it was decided that cities and churches and theatres would somehow combine to put on various types of entertainment including dances and movies. Only uniformed troops would be allowed in, and their friends. All such entertainment had to be wholesome, and was to close early enough to allow the troops to get back to their camps in a timely manner.

PRUNES IN THE HEADLINES

Doubtless every reader by now is desperate to find out what is happening to **prune marketing** in the nation. Well, below is a Letter that tells you all you need to know.

Letters, May Munro, Killara. Where have all the prunes gone? Should not there be some left over for all the babies requiring them? Prunes are most important in the young baby's diet as a natural medicine, and it seems rather unfair that mothers should be at their wits' end trying, hopelessly, to find a substitute.

RELAXATION OF BROWN-OUT RULES

It was announced today by the SES that trams, buses and trains would now be allowed to travel at night without restrictions of their internal lighting. Masks required on private cars will be eased considerably in the next few days.

Comment. Remember Mr Pettit's above Letter.

MAY NEWS ITEMS

Pillaging on Sydney's wharf has reached serious proportions. So much so that police inspected labourers as they left work yesterday, and charged 14 of them with stealing. Police said that they had checked on only a small proportion of labourers, and that the result indicated the practice of stealing was widespread, and of such magnitude as to impact the nation's War effort.

Salvage authorities pointed out that aluminium and rubber were still wanted for munitions work. However, they emphasized that just as important were **rags, old clothing and waste paper**.

Mrs Brooks of Picton pointed out that **the humble weed dandelion**, when thoroughly dried in an electric oven, makes excellent **coffee**. Only the root is to be used. This can be most useful if the tea ration is not sufficient.

Ration books for the nation will be issued on June 14. They are adaptable, and can be used for clothing or for any other matter that it becomes necessary to ration. Citizens must produce their **new Identity Cards** to claim their ration books. These will be on issue in the next few days.

Mr Wilkins from Griffith comments that *God Save the Queen* is the National Anthem. He writes that he has no problem with it being played in theatres and other places of entertainment at the start of the show. He has no problem with standing to attention while this happens. But he is quite annoyed by having **this repeated at the**

end of the performance. It in no way improves morale or loyalty. It is just a device for the Government to impose its restrictive mentality on the people, and keep them from thinking for themselves. "If they act like sheep, they will think like sheep."

Letter-writers complained that **air-raid slit trenches**, across the nation, were full of water and **breeding** dengue mosquitoes.

Victory suits were not selling, said the Rationing Commission. It suggested that this was a "good thing" because the aim of rationing was to reduce consumption.

The Commonwealth Prices Commissioner has announced the **immediate increase in price of wax matches**.

Daylight saving was to start across the nation on Sunday 25th of September.

Wardens were increasingly getting frustrated by the apparent uselessness of their jobs. A writer, titled Warden, summed up this irritation. "Most of the wardens engaged in next Sunday's brown-out will see themselves as loitering for two hours without intent in a public place....

"We object to the **constant requests and directions coming from headquarters to attend meetings, carry out exercises, wait at posts or to patrol a brown-out** that the Minister himself admits he does not want."

Tarzan movies were doing well at the Box Office.

Abbott and Costello likewise.

MILITARY NEWS

The Japanese continued with their conquests in Burma. They were getting close to the boundary with India, and had penetrated a few hundred miles into China. The British forces in Burma were in a slow, bitterly-fought retreat, and nowhere in that region was there any sign that the Japs would be halted.

Closer to home, the gradual build up of American forces in and around Australia was stiffening our defence. In particular, air raids on the Jap-held territories in New Guinea were more frequent and more effective, and it seemed **we were breaking even in the air**. But having said that, at the end of the month, the number of air raids on Port Moresby reached 50.

But earlier in the month **an important battle took place. In the Coral Sea**, north east of New Guinea. The Japanese had assembled a huge force with the intention of moving round the eastern end of New Guinea by sea, and moving westward to capture Port Moresby. The Americans had about 20 major ships, including two air-craft carriers, and were deliberately trying to locate the Japanese. On May 8th, and for three days after, a huge naval battle ensued. In it, both sides lost a carrier, and each lost about 40 planes.

But it was **an important strategic victory for Australia**, because the Japanese learned, the hard way, that the capture of further territory in an invasion by sea would surely entail further dreadful losses. **The Japs never again attempted a sea-borne invasion of Australian territory.** But we did not know this at the time.

The news from the Coral Sea did little to relieve Australians from their fearful sense of dread. If they had realized the importance of that battle, they would have felt a **bit** better, but our propaganda machine thought it best to restrict our information to the bare bones. It was only later that the nation fully realised that this was a major turning point for Australia.

NEWS FROM EUROPE

Things were only middling in Europe. The Russians were locked in enormous battles wars along their Western front with Hitler's armies, re-enforced and well equipped after the Winter and the thaw. There was no doubt that Hitler was about to launch a massive counter-attack, and early indications, such as they were, suggested that the Germans had far more resources that did the Russians.

In the Atlantic, the enemy subs were still marauding with great success, and Britain was feeling desperate. In the Middle East, Rommel was gaining the upper hand. The Brits were always talking about opening up a Second Front on the west coast of Europe, or in North Africa, to divert German resources from the Russian Front. But it was slowly being realised that they could not do this in the current year. Britain seemed to be wandering with no clear purpose, and as a consequence, Churchill was under tough attack in Parliament and the Press.

CURTIN'S SPEECH

The Prime Minister, John Curtin, made a speech to the nation over radio of a Friday night on May 9th. Millions of Australians huddled over their living-room radios to hear any word about the Coal Sea battle that they suspected of being under way. Below are the dramatic words they heard.

I tell you bluntly that the whole world may well shake within the next few weeks under the blows that full-scale warfare will strike, and Australia cannot escape a blow.   Right now we face vital perilous weeks, fraught with exceedingly important happenings for Australia.   Invasion is a menace capable hourly of becoming a reality.

I have said, in the plainest words that without adequate air and naval support all talk of an offensive from this country is meaningless.   We want to strike, we know how to strike, but our striking power must have behind it the full strength of the nation.   Our punch must be loaded with everything Australia has behind it.

Everything means no subtractions, no excuses, no reservations, no subterfuges. Organisation on the home front will be imposed, so that anyone who wants to escape the responsibility involved will be caught up either as individuals or as groups. **The home front economy is our second fighting line,** and every citizen is in the fighting line, no less than the uniformed man in the front line.

The nation has made no real sacrifices of peace-time things.   The Government tells you the time has come when we can no longer avoid sacrifice, and that you must end, and **will** sacrifice, those peace-time things.

Mr Curtin went on to announce that rationing of clothing would be introduced soon. In the meantime, from tomorrow, sales of clothing, blankets and Manchester would be controlled down to 75 per cent of the previous week's total.

His message continued: I say to you quite flatly that regard will be given only to the minimum requirements of the civilian population. That is, we aim to use a bare minimum. We must understand it is not what we want, it's what we can have from now on. If we fail to adjust our way of living accordingly, then we not only render a national disservice as individuals, but we endanger our fighting men and the security of our country.

Forget about that new hat to match the material you have bought. A blue shirt will cover you – don't think about buying a grey shirt to match a grey suit. **A darning needle is a weapon of war these days**. Use it on your old clothes. **Don't buy new things.**

With your co-operation the Government's reduction of 25 per cent can be greatly increased, and there is no reason why purchases cannot be reduced by 30 per cent, or 40, or even 50 per cent, during the next few years.

What we have to do is fight for, to work for, to save Australia as a nation. What we do for Australia now is what Australia needs for its preservation. Never was a greater call made to any people. I am convinced beyond all doubt that you, the great-minded patriotic people of our great and proud Australia, will answer that call with strength, with purpose, and with high resolve.

Comment. This was a great speech, delivered with a sincerity and the self-effacement that had endeared him to the nation. I am sure that almost everyone supported Curtin in these, and subsequent, calls for austerity. But, as usual, when it got down to implementation, things fell apart, for a time.

THE DARNING NEEDLE REALLY IS HERE

The job of introducing clothing rationing to Australia fell to the Minister for War Organisation of Industry, John Dedman. He was already unpopular with the masses because of his dithering, and his wisdom was always under question. He was called "The Minister for Austerity" by his many detractors.

It is fair to say that, in introducing clothing rationing, he lived up to his dubious reputation. Every one of his decisions seemed to rile large sections of the population. **For example**, he placed no controls on **when s**hops could sell their now-limited supplies. So the shops opened each day, blissfully selling for only an hour until they met their quota. But there were millions of people, all in jobs, who could not get to the shops at that time. When did they buy?

The populace was furious. Part of their irritation was because they were being rationed in the first place. But beyond that, the innate mix of regulations and non-regulations in this interim period was driving them crazy. Letters poured in. **In the first instance**, they abused Dedman and his shoot-from-the-hip policy decisions. After a few days of chaos in the shops, **panic buying** really set in, so **the second wave** of Letters was critical of all things concerned with the panic. Later, in about a month, **a third wave** agonised over the weaknesses of the rationing system and the distribution of the goods. In all, there was plenty to criticise.

Here, in the middle of this fiasco, I will content myself with publishing five Letters that all appeared across two days in the *SMH*. I think they speak for themselves.

Letters, Digger's Father. The panic buying serves to illustrate how utterly useless it is to appeal to the better nature of the community. It demonstrates the utter selfishness and greed of citizens to whom it is a waste of time to appeal for their co-operation in facing the horrors of war. The response of frantic shoppers to the Prime Minister's request that they conserve and save, shows how low our so-called democracy has sunk with everybody playing for his or her own hand. The indecent manner in which the stores were mobbed, and in which people bought up more than their fair share of goods offering, is proof of the lack of spiritual and moral values at the base of our community life, and reveals our shallowness and superficial loyalty to the cause of democracy. While millions of oppressed and enslaved men, women, and children are dying and suffering throughout conquered Europe, bereft of homes, adequate clothing, food, and medical care, these moronic elements of our own race rush, in a mad scramble, to assure their own selfish needs and comforts. May God help us!

Letters, A Soldier's Mother. Sydney can't take it! I view the shops and read the papers with utter disgust as I note the panic buying.

Ration cards do not mean "no clothes." We shall all get our share, and if we are shabby, what of it? Nice homes and clothes appeal to us all, but this is war, and to win it means everything. Money cannot buy freedom and liberty; without them life would not be worth living.

Our loved ones are bleeding for us. A great naval battle has been fought not far from our coastline, and may flare up again. Yet in Australia the people are mobbing shops for clothes!

What reading will this make for our boys who have given up home and loved ones to fight for freedom – undergoing untold hardships for us all! Australians, where is your loyalty and patriotism? Where is your conscience?

Letters, A Mere Tracer. One reads with cynical humour Mr Dedman's statement that the clothes rationing system "is now working satisfactorily." I would invite Mr Dedman to come with us on a shopping excursion. First, the office girl who needs one more skein of wool to finish the winter woollies for her aged, invalid mother, sallies forth at lunch-time to purchase it, and is told at all stores, "Sorry, our quota is sold for to-day; we open at 9am tomorrow!" The underwear counter report is the same, so she cannot buy ready-mades to serve for the time.

Secondly, the salesgirl who has to support her mother is dismissed on account of the rationing. Hundreds of salesgirls now find themselves out of employment. No doubt these will eventually be employed on munitions, but who will pay the bills in the interval? If Mr Dedman stood in our shoes and knew what it was to be cold and hungry, would he still think "the system was now working satisfactorily?"

Letters, Ruth Beale. We have had another amusing exhibition of a Federal Minister stampeding the public. The desire to be the one to "say something" by persons unused to the conducting of big business is the cause, and when the effect is a mess the blame is shifted to the women who take advantage of the ill-considered talk.

If one looks at the crowds of shoppers, they are not the ordinary customers of any given big store, but the bargain-sales crowd which usually appears twice a year, which is made up of poor people or thrifty mothers and daughters with small allowances who usually wear last year's clothes until this year's sales. There are also the customers who have to buy during the winter holidays the clothes their growing children need for next term. Furthermore, there are families who have not had regular pay-envelopes since the depression of Lang's Government, and now for the first time they can be fully clothed.

But there are persons in the crowds plainly black-market buyers, the enemies of governments, services, and housewives, and to them no mercy should be shown.

Letters, Merchant. Do not the present woeful exhibitions give cause for deep thought of the possibility of what might eventuate under a more serious circumstance in time of crisis? If we people cannot control ourselves to better effect at times like these, and our leaders cannot display a little more of the intelligent qualities expected of them, are we not faced with the risk of repetition of that sad exhibition of panic and stampede which overtook France two years ago.

Comment. These were all strong Letters. The last one, by Merchant, probably best reflects the mood of many of the population. These people went along with Curtin's call to sacrifice, and accepted the necessity for rationing of clothes and other materials. They were quite happy to complain time and time again, but they were at the same time very happy to be living in a country where they could do just that. Curtin had their support. Dedman, on the other hand, won few friends and, as the War progressed, it was he who became the most reviled politician in the nation, despite having quite a few competitors for that honour.

MORALS: AN OPINION

News item. Address to the NSW Presbyterian Assembly by the Right Rev C F D McAlpine, Moderator.

"We are living in an age where sin is blatant and evil flaunts itself," he said. "This moral decadence and the gross materialism of today have caused a blight to fall on everything with which man has to do. Included in this stricture, music, and pictorial art have reflected a lower moral tone. It may be said there is no need to listen if you don't like the broadcast, but what if the neighbouring wireless are sets out of one's control?

"There has been a serious drift, a throwback as it were, to the savagery of the jungle. As for the songs, there is very little poetry in the words and very little sense. In the cinema the people are given what they want, implying that public taste is of a low order."

He added: "It must be admitted that many achieve an elegance and refinement wholly satisfying, and make us not ashamed of the women of our land, but on the other hand, some of the costumes worn in the public streets are so vulgar and audacious that one wonders at the brazen effrontery of the wearer. "I do not pretend to understand the significance of some of the terms used in the world of women, but until someone more sophisticated enlightens me I can only conclude that a 'glamour girl' is one loaded with vanity and outward display, and that 'sex appeal' is the process by which not only the unbalanced male, but the balanced male, may be stirred to unholy emotions."

Comment. This Moderator should consider himself lucky that he lived when he did. If he was present **now**, 80-odd years later, he would have plenty to add. Take the current crop of young strumpets moving round the world of entertainment and glamour. On the face of it, he would have plenty to talk about. Yet, behind these self-serving exhibitionists, and their multitude of Facebook followers, there is **another** multitude of sensible, wonderful and well-educated young people who are probably more balanced and better equipped to keep the world going than we were a generation or two ago. As usual, it's a great mish-mash, an endless mixture of the good and the bad, of the sane and the ratbag. **In essence, I suppose, it's just like real life.**

JUNE NEWS ITEMS

Whoops. The Minister for the Army stated that private boats that had been taken over and impounded would be **handed back to their owners.** Owners willing to reclaim their boats would need to sign a declaration that they would not pursue the Government for any damages done. It was commented by others that given that **much damage had been occasioned to many boats**, this would become a matter for further deliberation.

The Department of Supply yesterday appealed to **all holders of wheat sacks and chaff bags** to return them to their suppliers to relieve the present shortage.

Official clothing rationing started Monday June 15. By Friday June 19, officers of the Director of Rationing in NSW said they expected to have about **300,000 enquiries and complaints t**o respond to as soon as they could.

The NSW Minister for Education said yesterday that, because of the shortage of men, **women teachers would be posted to boys' high schools f**or the first time.

A Reverend Churchward from Beecroft called for ration coupons to be issued for **the consumption of alcohol.**

A "leading authority" (censored) on the **dairy industry in NSW** said last night that at least **500 farms in the State had closed down,** and the stock on others had been reduced by 20 to 30 per cent. This was because our efficient man-power has gone to munition works and the Services.

THE WORLD AROUND US

These were scary times in Australia. If you thought at the beginning of the month that the coming of the Yanks had turned the tide for us, you were quickly disappointed. In the first two weeks of the month, four Jap submarines crept into Sydney Harbour one night, sank a ferry and killed a dozen people. They did little damage, and were quickly destroyed, but **the psychological effect of the entry was devastating**.

In the next few weeks, the Japs sank a few merchant vessels off Sydney, and chased a few others. A bit later, a parent ship shelled the Eastern Suburbs from miles out on the ocean, and a few subs attacked Newcastle from within its harbour. For the average citizen right across the nation, these were very worrying incidents indeed.

On the oceans, the US forces had a major victory at the island of Midway, a few thousand miles from Australia's shores. The Japanese fleet had massed for a major attack on the east Pacific, including Hawaii, and were joined in battle by the American fleet. After some dubious hours, the Americans had a major victory, and this confirmed the message from the Coral Sea, but even more emphatically. In retrospect, many commentators see this as the turning point of the Pacific War, and argue that Japan's expansion came to a halt after this crippling defeat.

In Europe, the German subs were still picnicking, and on the ground Britain was shaken by the victories of the Germans in Libya. Tobruk was the mainstay of the British defence of the Suez Canal, because it was the most obvious place to land a German army and prepare it for an attack on Egypt. For months, the Brits and Empire troops had held Tobruk, and fought many battles across Libya defending their position. Suddenly, the Germans broke through and wiped out the resistance around Tobruk, and the Brits had to evacuate. They re-set their battle-lines on Egyptian soil.

The defeat in Lybia was sorely felt in Britain. They had been fed a steady diet of good news from the region, and now they reacted with shock. Then they found out that our two-pounder guns were no match for the German six-pounders, and that the German tanks were scarcely damaged by them. The incompetence of British leadership seemed apparent, and the public and Press were screaming for scapegoats. Churchill and his Cabinet had many hours of discomfort in Parliament, and only **escaped lynching** because it was impossible to find a better leader on the spot.

THE HALF-TIME SCORE

Now that half the year has gone, it seems appropriate to do a summing up. The last six months had seen such a huge change in Australian society that the "before" and "after" seem hard to correlate. We had been a care-free, cavalier, fun-loving society with a belief that war would never touch our shores, and we were now scared stiff that in only a few weeks the Japs would be sending tanks down our main streets.

Society was now fairly close to a full war footing, with rationing being progressively introduced, brown-outs being enforced, profits being restricted, buildings hard to build, prunes hard to buy, and farmers having no petrol to bring their crops to market. All sorts of regulations had been imposed on all civilians, a fair percentage of which made sense, and an **equal number that were imposed to meet the ego and political aspirations of a few would-be demigods**.

Equally, as the regulations were enforced locally, it was obvious that some of the enforcers were power-hungry, or near-idiots, or ignorant, and so there was a never-ending stream of complaints about the silliness of the new rules.

But **for the bulk of the population**, quietly bunkered down at home, **the war was now a reality**, and there was a serious threat of imminent invasion, and so they were very **prepared to do what they could** to prevent that. So, most of the men-folk had joined the services or were in volunteer corps of various kinds. Or they were working long hours in the large number of munitions or aircraft-manufacturing factories, or they were toiling in so-called protected jobs. Women had continued to perform all sorts of traditional duties such as the invaluable Red Cross, and fund raising committees.

But an increasing number were now employed as drivers of military vehicles or as signalers with the Forces, and in munitions factories. In all, **despite some conspicuous slackers**, the call for the country to mobilise had been well heeded.

The most depressing aspect of all, coupled with the worry of invasion, was the **non-stop reports of death, serious injury, and capture of our Servicemen by the enemy**. Every day, the papers carried an extensive list of the men affected, and every day it was substantial. The Department of Information could put out all the reports it wanted that said "Japanese planes attacked Port Moresby (or Darwin or in Burma). We had only three light casualties. Eight enemy aircraft were destroyed". But everyone now realised that such reports were completely false. They realised **that what was not false** were the casualty reports, and they had reached such proportions that each and every person in Australia knew someone that knew someone who had been thus affected.

What the man and woman in the street also realised was the depth of suffering felt by the families of the casualties. Beautiful silly young men, and sensible mature older men, sent off to be killed or maimed or captured in their thousands. The families left behind had to contemplate this, day after day, and hope the postman, day after day, would stay away from their letter-box. But there was also the worry for those families whose sons had not been yet reported. They might be, or they might not be, in some particular theatre of war, and they might be in danger. There was such uncertainty, such a nagging worry. All they could do was wait, and hope that the letter that did next arrive would be from their man, and **not from the Army**.

CAN WE AVOID INVASION?

Every person had their own answer to this question. **The pessimists had some very good arguments.** For example, they cited the recent losses in Russia and Libya, the continued loss of ships in the Atlantic. Should we put our faith in the British leaders who were responsible for these losses? They presume to either give or not give to

Australia the resources that were rightfully ours, yet their incompetence was everywhere for all to see.

They also argued that the Japanese had so many bases within striking distance of Australia that they were only days from sending their navy to subdue us. How could we defend such a vast continent with so few soldiers? Had not the Japs just entered Sydney Harbour last month, and this month had they not bombarded Newcastle, and attacked shipping only a few miles from Sydney? Was not our own Prime Minister constantly saying that a Japanese attack was more than possible, in the immediate future?

The optimists grasped at a series of little straws. Reports of the Naval victories in the Coral Sea and at Midway were most encouraging (if they could be believed). America was clearly sending in many more troops and planes quickly, and we could see in our own streets and skies that this was true. Our air raids on New Guinea and the like were doubtless taking some toll, (though it had to be admitted that the Jap counter-attacks on our northern cities, like Darwin and Port Moresby, had not eased). But our increased supply of planes and now some pilots back from Britain appeared to be paying off, and we were likely to have gained parity in the air. If this was so, then that was good news indeed.

So, the optimists and pessimists argued back and forth. The whole thing was even more confused by the now-certain knowledge that we were only being told half the truth, and that **no one at all**, not even John Curtin, **was getting the full picture.** Mind you, as history later revealed, no one even in Japan was at all clear on whether an invasion would be attempted at the time, so we were not alone in our ambivalence on the matter.

BURYING DEAD JAPANESE SAILORS

The Jap sailors who died in the submarine attacks had been buried here with full military honours. Arrangements had been made to send their ashes back to Japan. The question arose as to whether we should be doing this, or whether we should adopt tougher measures. Some people were saying that we were getting reports of Japanese brutality both in battle, and in prison camps, and also of their cruelty to the civilian populations they had conquered. Surely then, they argued, we should treat **their dead** the same way that they were treating **our living**, that is without any trace of humanity or sympathy.

Letters, W Lennard. In 1843 Afghan tribesmen wiped out a small body of eleven English soldiers. It was the custom of these Mohammedans to tie a red thread round the wrist of any tribesman who died fighting bravely. When Napier and his forces found the dead eleven, there was a crimson thread tied round both wrists of each Briton!

During the Matabele War, Major Wilson and a number of British soldiers were surrounded and killed at the Shangani River. It was the custom of the Matabeles to mutilate the bodies of their enemies slain in battle. But when Lobengula surveyed the field he said: "Let them be. They were men, men who died like men, men whose fathers were men!"

There seems to be a great contrast between the ideas of these **savages** and those who say we should treat the fallen Japs in an uncivilised manner. Personally I greatly prefer the Afghan and the Matabele point of view.

Letters, P E B. Sickening passages in the diary taken from a dead Japanese officer, published by your correspondent who was in Burma, must lead many Australians to share the view of the general secretary of the ANA. Respectful burial of the enemy's dead, as has been pointed out, is a civilised practice common to most belligerents, but does this include the Japanese? Surely not. Reports of atrocities are becoming more frequent. Can we expect after such atrocities that the obsequies are conducted with Service honours? "We found the body of a British lieutenant strung from a tree for all to see," says the Japanese officer's diary. "Many jokes were made." Another abhorrent passage shows how barbarous is our enemy. "Our battery commander received a burst of bullets in the stomach. For this a prisoner of war was killed.

First Hosogawa bayoneted him in the back, which gave the men much amusement. Then he stuck him in the belly. He didn't die at once, but, of course, it is not permitted to waste bullets when killing prisoners of war." These were military atrocities.

Letters, E Sheldon. The dead Japanese seamen recovered from the submarines displayed heroism reflecting nothing but credit upon them, chances of survival being almost nil. I think that most naval men, whilst mourning their comrades, will at the same time readily pay tribute to the gallantry of their enemy, which they did at the graveside. What amazed Mr Redding, of the ANA, is that we should have paid this courtesy to Japanese nationals against whom a few weeks ago we were directing the most puerile and nonsensical vituperation, which we misnamed propaganda. Let us remember that reports of our treatment of any Japanese who may fall into our hands, dead or alive, cannot help but influence our enemy in her treatment of our lads in their hands, some of whom may find their last resting place in their country.

Editor's Note, *SMH*. Many more letters, on both sides of this debate, have been received than can possibly be published. The correspondence cannot be continued.

CLOTHES RATIONING IS HERE AT LAST

Clothes rationing details were released to the public. Men and women were each to be issued with 112 coupons that were to cover all purchases for a year. It was estimated officially that a man's three-piece suit of trousers, vest, and coat would take 38 coupons. A shirt would take 12, shoes 12, and a hat 5. Women's overcoats were 19, corsets 6, petticoats 5, and gloves 3, stockings 4, and bloomers 4. Handkerchiefs and handbags were coupon free. Repairs to footwear were also coupon free, and so too was mending-wool not exceeding half an ounce.

The process of introducing rationing was hardly trouble-free. Letters on the matter were prolific.

Letters, H Graythwaite. I wish to draw attention to a most glaring and audacious misinterpretation – or, if not, it is an outrageous piece of injustice – of this new Rationing Act. Apparently, he who has made a lay-by before a certain date, is, quite justly, allowed to collect and pay for it up to the end of July without coupons; whereas he who has bought and paid for **material** months ago, and had it made up by a tailor, apparently, merely because **the suit** is not finished by Monday next, owing to war-time delays, will have to surrender his coupons, just as if he had made the purchase next week. How can you make fish of one, and flesh of another in that fashion?

Letters, Home Dressmaker. A casual glance at the coupon allowance for ready garments and dress materials shows that the thrifty housewife, the mother who makes her own and her children's clothes, has had no consideration whatever. Apparently the coupon allowance list has been made up on the advice of manufacturers solely, and the woman who purchases her own material and makes up her own frocks has been left out in the cold. A dress length of winter woolen material, of which approximately three yards are needed, requires 15 coupons: but the ready-made article can be obtained with 13 coupons!

One idea of the coupon rationing, as detailed by the Department was to release people from factories in order that they could go into munitions. People would be forced to make their own clothes, and for that reason haberdashery – needles, threads, etc., were coupon free. Now more people than ever will be employed in the factories as ready-mades require less coupons than the material itself!

There is a call for immediate and drastic alteration. Materials required by the home dressmaker should not cost (in coupons) any more than half the price of the ready-made article. When coupon values were being arranged the executives of women's domestic associations should have been called in for advice.

Letters, Constant Knitter. I wonder has the Rationing Commission thought of the effect upon the comforts of our fighting forces. Like many other women, I have knitted since September, 1939, and to date have made and delivered to comforts funds **over 3300 pairs of socks, together with numerous pullovers, balaclavas, etc.** Any knitter will know this represent over 1,200 ounces of wool, or in rationing language, 600 coupons, in less than three years.

Willing and able as I am to keep at what is clearly my duty, my coupon rations entirely prevent it, for even if I knit but one pair of socks a week I would require to give up 100 coupons in the year. Surely all khaki or navy wool for such purposes should be excluded from the coupon rationing system.

Letters, Joseph Evans. As a salesman in the juvenile section of a large city retail store, I would like to point to the inconsistency of Mr Coles' statement that the chief burden of the rationing plan will fall on those best able to bear it, i.e. adults. Flannelette pyjamas for infants having a maximum outside leg measurement of 24in rates six coupons, stock sizes for children of 3-4 years exceeds this measurement, which places them in the coupon rating of a youth 14-15 years, i.e. 10 coupons.

Secondly, no provision has been made for infants of 3-4 years for shirts in the lower rating: once again these infants are placed in the 14-15 years rating, i.e., seven coupons per shirt. This represents 25 per cent of the total coupon rating for four shirts.

For good measure with the above omission, Mr Dedman has seen fit to place no coupon rating on braces, both children's and men's, which contain latex, silk, cotton, leather, and metals, all of which have long since been placed on the list of essentials in war industry.

The planners appear to have used the commodity unit basis rather than the more equitable basis of durability and quality. Example: One singlet retailed at 2/11 rates the same coupon value as one retailed at 19/6. Therefore, lower incomes are penalised through their inability to purchase goods of a durable quality and they are compelled to use a greater number of coupons, which seems to defeat the social justness of the plan.

ABSENTEEISM IN INDUSTRY

Workers in factories producing war goods were working long hours, and generally six shifts a week. While this was good for their finances, it was taking its toll on their heath and stamina.

Letters, 1,300 Times An Hour. Your sub-leader on factory absenteeism was appropriate enough, but some of us factory workers are full up with much of the cant and humbug published on this subject.

I have not lost any time through illness or weariness because I know enough to save myself in some degree from both these very human weaknesses. Factory workers are not articulate, but let me describe a few facts. Any psychologist could explain why absenteeism must inevitably result: the curious thing is that those whose business is should be to know something of industrial psychology seem quite ignorant of the real reason for absenteeism and (in our case) the absurdly high rate of labour turnover and general readiness to seek a rest by striking over trifles.

We have no rest periods or refreshments in our annexe. We work 7½ hours, and are paid for eight hours daily; the only refreshment or rest allowed is in the middle of the shift. We work three round-the-clock shifts. Our wages, if twice as high, would not compensate some of us for what in time inevitably becomes physical, nervous, or mental torture.

The torture arises from the noise and vibration from machinery, the weariness and fatigue resulting from repetition work without rest periods or refreshment. I use three machines, on one using both hands, both feet, and eyes, treading the pedal 6,600 times, 1,100 motions (both hands and eyes) on each of two other machines – total, 8,800 motions or operations in 7½ hours, nearly 1,200 an hour. The rate is actually higher, for temporary rests must be stolen on some excuse.

I work six shifts a week, and am often called on to work overtime in four-hour shifts.

Any critic can have my job. I would prefer the front line trenches if I could get there. I feel I could enjoy that.

THE FALL-OUT FROM SUNDAY SHOWS

The heated discussions, about providing Sunday entertainment for the troops, were just about over. Some Protestant Churches and many conservatives had wanted no such entertainment at all, but they had to be content with the various compromises that had been reached across the nation. Still, they were not daunted at all, and were quite vocal in stating where they stood on public morals.

For example the Presbyterian Church, at an Assembly in Newcastle, roundly condemned any form of gambling. It urged that the NSW Government should **abandon the State Lottery**, despite the subsequent loss of revenue, supposedly for hospitals. **It condemned alcohol**, and urged the Federal Government to prohibit the manufacture of alcohol as a **beverage.** Light entertainment on Sundays was acceptable, but no form of public entertainment should be permitted. Any move to allow **commercial interests to partake should be forbidden**. Current proposals to force 2CH, a popular Church-sponsored radio station, to **accept adverts** from **any** sponsor should be "opposed to the death by the Church as a dictatorial interference with the liberty of conscience."

JULY NEWS ITEMS

The Army was concerned about the **large scale theft** and re-selling **of its petrol**. Thus it added a secret compound to its supplies which, by the use of a simple re-agent, identified that the petrol was owned by the Army.

The Minister for Trade announced that henceforth consumers would be able to buy half a pound of tea **(eight ounces)** every five weeks, instead of the **current five ounces**....

Henceforth customers **will not need to register with a licensed tea-supplier**, but may buy their tea from any supplier simply by producing their coupons....

Customers in restaurants and cafes will be able to purchase **a single cup of tea,** but no top-ups.

Individuals wishing to **send clothing and linens to laundries** will be able to do so **once a fortnight**. Deliverers will be restricted to allocated areas so that they cover a particular area only once a fortnight.

The Leader of the NSW Opposition today advocated **a food-rationing scheme in Australia**. He said that we in Australia should go short of some food so that **more could be sent to Britain**.

The Minister for War Organisation, Mr Dedman, announced that the **dry cleaning of many articles of clothing** would in future not be allowed. These includes men's suits and dinner suits and cream trousers, and evening frocks for women. He also included all furnishings....

Mr Dedman also announced that certain types of meat would be in short supply. He recom**mended that the civilian population should eat more mutton**, so the other types of meat can go to our servicemen.

The Womens' Employee Board decided that women in munitions factories doing work previously done by men should be paid at **90 per cent of the male wage**. The small difference was because women would not be asked to do **heavy lifting**, and carrying jobs, and similar work.

A gentleman writing from Manly reminded Army officers that, when on leave, they must always **return the salutes of soldiers of lower ranks**. He pointed out that the salute was to give honour, not to the man, but to the rank.

It was expected that **50 thousand boy scouts** would collect waste rubber, door-to-door, next weekend.

The Federal Minister for Supply appealed to the population to give up their thousands of **unused or worn-out hot-water bottles** for re-use.

Primary industries were suffering needlessly because of delays in releasing men **temporarily from the Armed Services for work on their home farms,** claimed a Victorian MP. The Army had approved the new regulations, but it seemed not to have gotten through to the Army administrators.

WAR NEWS

Russia had now been in the War for just on a year. Before that, Stalin and Hitler had been locked into treaties with each other that agreed that Russia would provide food and raw materials for Germany, and in return Germany would supply them with war equipment. This was a handy relationship for both parties, and Stalin was quite happy with it.

But not so Hitler. He had an abiding hatred of Communism, and the so-called Jewish influence in Russia. Accordingly, a year ago, in **one of the greatest blunders of his War**, he invaded that massive country, with its huge population and vast natural resources.

Comment. The size of that population was brought home by Stalin pointing out, **on the anniversary of the start of the Russian War**, that the nation had **four and a half million casualties in that year**. That included men who were killed and injured too badly to return to fighting, POW's, and deserters. No matter which way I look at that figure, I can't comprehend it. It is too big, too monstrous, too degrading to humanity, for me to take in.

Right now however, the situation for Russia was looking very grim. On all three fronts, the massive German summer campaign was grinding its way, painful mile after painful mile, into Russian territory, and the slaughter on both sides was terrible. In Britain and Washington, there were again loud cries for the Allies to **open a second front** to draw the Germans away from Russia. But it was clearly too soon, and Britain had its own new troubles in the Middle East. So Russia was left to carry its own burden in the fighting.

Britain's trouble stemmed from the loss of Tobruk, and the advance of Rommel's force into North Africa. His targets were obviously the Egyptian capital, Cairo, and Alexandria at the entrance to the Suez Canal. Fierce fighting started at the beginning of the month, and by the end it was just as fierce. It seemed, from news reports, which might or might not have been reliable, that the Brits and Aussies were getting slightly the better of it. But the end result was very much in doubt, and Churchill and his Cabinets were under constant scrutiny by Parliament.

THE AUSSIE FRONT

Things were a bit quieter in the Pacific. The Japs were still chasing the tail end of the British out of Burma. They were also having sporadic wins in China, but not as easily as before. The entry of American air planes into the fray was undoubtedly having a marked effect, and there were suggestions here and there that **maybe** the Japanese had extended themselves too far in their rapid advances. **Maybe,** after gaining all that territory, their lines of supply were too long, and the business of administering and controlling them was weighing on their man-power. **Maybe** the drubbings that they had taken in the Coral Sea and Midway were making their Navy re-think their desire for further conquests. **In any case**, July was a more reassuring month for Australians.

That is not to say there were no incidents. Towards the end of the month, Port Hedland in Western Australia was bombed for the first time. And on the east coast, Townsville too was raided. Then, in the last few days, the Japs landed a smallish number of troops at each of a few points on the **north coast of New Guinea**.

Would they actually try to take over the Australian territory of New Guinea? Would they try to fight their way over the 60 miles of the Owen Stanley Ranges to capture Port Moresby? If they did try, where should we meet them in combat? There was only one decent track across the Ranges, and it passed through an unknown place called Kokoda. Perhaps on that track? No one had any answers to these questions at this stage, so I suggest we wait a while and see if anything does happen there.

THIS IS THE NEWS FROM THE ABC

News broadcasts from the ABC were very important. There was no TV, and commercial Stations did not have the resources to provide their own news services. So, the news from the ABC was eagerly heard every day at 7am, 12.30 pm, and 7 pm. Some die-hards waited up till 10pm to hear the news from the BBC, and many also tuned into broadcasts from Berlin and Tokyo on static-ridden Short Wave. In 1942, one of the enduring pictures of the times is the sight of entire families leaning over the radio in the lounge-room, listening for news of the Japs.

Only a few months ago, when the Japanese forces were advancing at such a fantastic pace toward Australia, the Australian Broadcasting Commission changed its news bulletins format to cater for the public interest in **news from the Pacif**ic. That means that it put Oz news first, before overseas news. **Now**, by July, world focus was on Russia, and whether it would be over-run. And on England, and whether it could save Egypt and the Canal. Both of these were on a knife-edge.

The trouble here was that the ABC, doubtless in conjunction with the Department of Information, was not only keeping the Oz component of the news to forefront, but it had expanded it to include about 15 minutes of guff from various Ministers who were intent on publicising the own war-winning sets of regulations. It was only after that, that the brief news from the battle-fronts came through.

Most people were exasperated with the refusal of officialdom to tell us what was really happening, and for many, the ABC's refusal to change was a red rag to the bulls. .

Letters, N Hugill. There is demand on every side that the oversea news should be read before the so-called Australian news on the ABC national programme. For months now we have had to listen to the parish pump items from Canberra, in which no one is interested at this critical stage of the war, before being told of the world-shaking events for which our ears are tuned.

I am an Australian of the fourth generation, and I consider it an insult to my intelligence to suggest, by offering them first, that most items of "Australian" news have more significance than the real war news which follows. Here is a sample: How much a day we are spending on the war – the value of carrots as a diet for the armed forces – the squabble over the abuse of the security regulations – and so on. Why divide the news anyway? Why can't we simply have the "news" arranged by someone who knows news value in its real sense – and read by someone who does not find it necessary to emphasise many unimportant words.

Letters, Listener.   One evening this week we waited with what patience we could muster to 16 minutes' of burble about the fixed price of carrots, and views held by Cabinet Ministers, who took this opportunity of being in the news, whilst our hearts and minds were insistent in their demands for news of the battles being fought in Egypt and Russia. Is this not another reason for a national Government? Then the best brains of the country might not so insult our intelligence.

Letters, (Rev) E Pitcher.   One Monday at 7pm "Australian News" was read for 15 minutes. In this news the humble potato received honourable mention. But in the mind of everyone was the question, "Does the line still hold in Egypt?" On Tuesday, in 13 minutes of Canberra news, the price of unwashed carrots was rated of more importance than whether Russia held the new German offensive!

During a debate in the recent Newcastle Synod, Professor Elkin recalled that on the night in which Singapore fell, an anxious nation was informed that the sausage might be threatened with nudity.

Surely, it is time for our leaders to recover from the panic into which events threw them and to restore our news services to their normal proportions? The ABC has seemed strangely indifferent to public desire in this matter.

Letters, Indignant Aussie. We all realise how important the oversea news is, but, surely, any real Australian is more interested the news items of his own country than in foreign affairs. How would the people of England feel if our news was read before their own – most indignant, I wager. Your correspondent states that "no one is interested in the so-called Australian news." To us the Australian news is the most important event on the ABC. It would be a mistake, indeed, if we were all well informed as regards foreign affairs, but ignorant of our home matters.

Letters, H R. The protests against the system of having an Australian "session" before the war news and news of the world must have the sympathy of the majority of Australian listeners. Of what interest will be the Australian news if the Nazi-Fascist hordes over-run Europe? Let better sense prevail in these days of anxiety: what is actually happening to hundreds of millions of our allies should take precedence of what might happen to eight million people in Australia.

Letters, (Miss) H Sommerville. Let me add my protest against the piffle which passes as "Australian News from Canberra." Surely the limit was reached this morning when, at the 7.45 session, with the fate of the whole world hanging in the balance, listeners were treated to a solid twelve minutes of items of such vital interest as an account of a farewell party tendered by one Parliamentarian to another, before the real news was given. Cannot the newly-constituted Broadcasting Commission see that something is done to remedy this deplorable state of affairs? Personally, I consider the suggestion of one of your correspondents that the news to be broadcast be edited with relation to its value by someone who really knows news an excellent one.

WAR CASUALTIES

Every day now the newspapers were printing official lists, issued by the Armed Forces,that contained the names of men who had become casualties of the War. Those men who had been killed and permanently injured were included, and also those missing as POW's. Known deserters were not included as such. There was scant information, and even the specific theatre of war was not published. Letters sent to families contained only this same very basic information, though sometimes, depending on the fashion of the time, they did include the theatre.

This was very hard on many POW families, because often they did not know **where** their boys were detained. There was often a big difference between being held by the Germans and being subject to the Japanese Army.

The list on names was heart-rending. **Column after column** of names, and ranks and a rough indication of whether they were dead, or injured, or just prisoners of war. Many people said this was heartless, but no one suggested a better system. Every family with men overseas suffered from anxiety day after day, until for some, the bad news was confirmed, and then they suffered even more.

INTRODUCTION OF CLOTHES RATIONING

Needless to say, the introduction of clothes rationing had a few hitches. This is hardly surprising, given that seven million people had to be considered, and half of the nation's best work-force was in the army or co-opted elsewhere.

The introduction of **standardised clothing materials and styles gave everyone a shoc**k. For men, the only suit that would be available in future would be made from **a single standardised material,** and would no longer have a waist coat, or cuffs on the trousers. It would be single-breasted instead of double-breasted, belts on trousers were off the menu, and socks were now half-hose instead of full-hose. It was estimated that 113 Victory Suits could be made from the material previously used for 100 suits. There would be a limit of three pockets in men's trousers, and only two buttons would be allowed on coats.

Letters, R Clive Teece. From the description of the standardised cloth, it appears that this is to be made of **one uniform thickness**. Suits to be worn in the summer in Brisbane and Townsville are to be of the same thickness as those to be worn in winter in Melbourne and on the Monaro and New England tablelands. This is a typical example of the inefficiency which seems to be inseparable from Government control of industry.

MAN-POWER

As the idea of a war-economy gradually became more widely accepted, the Government became more ambitious in its targets. At this stage, it started talk about an extra 300,000 men for the armed services, and to wonder about where these men would come from. Perhaps from protected industry, perhaps from the current shirkers, perhaps by changing the age limits so as to enlist older men. Perhaps, given that some women were anxious to do their bit, more women could be used in factories and on the land. The subject was one of controversy, as the mixed bag of Letters below shows.

Letters, C Jones. A partial solution in finding the right class of men for the military or labour forces can be found in the combing of some of the large engineering firms doing Governmental work. Hundreds of young men, between the ages of 20 and 23, are today shirking their responsibilities and sheltering under the guise of essential services.

The men largely responsible for the trouble now being experienced at one of our naval yards are young men who would be much improved if they were forced to get into uniform and undergo some form of discipline, which, if one is drawn into contact with them, is seen to be entirely lacking. One has only to listen to their conversation to realise that they are completely devoid of the proper spirit, either national or civic, and unless the Government takes some stand to discipline this type of young man, our difficulties after are going to be manifold.

Letters, F A W. There is another aspect of this appeal which might be considered by the Director-General. Many of those who have retired have not done so of their own volition. They have reached the retiring age (what that is may vary) and perforce must give way to the men who are there to take their places as soon as they go.

They may be as fit as they were 4 or 5 years ago, but that is of no account. No move is made by the Director-General or his deputy to see that these men are medically examined when they reach that retiring age to ascertain whether they are fit to continue their work and so allow some of the younger men to enter the fighting forces.

Letters, Ex-Papuan RM and FRGS. I served in the last war from December, 1915, and at present am active and as fit and well as I was then. That is definite, for I have recently had a medical overhaul.

As an instructor, the Army admits my qualifications would be "valuable for training purposes," but, up to date, they have not decided to make use of my services.

I have applied for the Administration Branch of the RAAF, and stated that I was prepared to volunteer for home or oversea service, but they "cannot utilise" my services. Even although not a seaman I have applied for the RAN, but am informed I have "passed out of the age groups for enlistment."

As we have only 7,000,000 against Japan's 100,000,000, all this seems strange to me, especially as I am a certificated musketry instructor, have some special knowledge of topography and draftsmanship, know Papua and New Guinea from Torres Straits right around through Moresby, Samarai, and Rabaul, to the Anchorites, north of Maron, and, by virtue of the fact that I have patrolled for 22 years, know all there is to know about jungle, swamp, and mountain life and travel.

Not being a fitter, boilermaker, or tractor-driver, I cannot answer calls for jobs like that, so will now be forced to seek a purely civilian position.

Letters, A Hayward. When Curtin came into office no spokesman could make an announcement without referring to his party as "realists" and their policy as "realism"; yet they have since proved themselves hopeless idealists. The most glaring example is the Government's refusal to make use of suitable prisoners of war to relieve the acute shortage of labour in primary production.

International law permits the employment of prisoners on production not directly connected with the fighting forces, but even were this not so, the enemy has given us ample provocation to employ them in any capacity. In recent months captured Imperial troops have been forced to handle cargo under RAF bombing at Benghazi and the Japanese announced that the Port of Singapore had been restored by "captured Empire troops," including, no doubt, our own men. The "Herald" reports that Germany in addition to her own immense man-power is employing 2,500,000 "foreign workers" and 1,500,000 "working prisoners of war", yet this country of 7,000,000 not only refuses to engage its prisoners on useful and peaceful production, but is actually about to release some of its small army to form mobile labour squads.

I have no doubt that efficient and willing workers at any type of primary labour could be found in the prison camps (especially Italian) to form these squads, which could be guarded by garrison battalions. Even if it were necessary **to placate the unions by granting their absurd demands to pay these men award wages,** the scheme should be started as soon as possible, for the day is fast approaching to decide whether we or the Japanese will in future eat the produce of this country.

Letters, O Bissett. No one surely can claim that a male radio announcer is a very essential person, yet there are numbers of young single men employed by radio stations and theatrical companies, all apparently exempt. One sees pictures in the papers every week of young boxers and football players, and I know that the enormous number of fit-looking men in mufti to be seen every day in the streets and restaurants is a source of bewilderment t.

Letters, M Bruxner, NSW Legislative Assembly. A friend of mine felt that he should leave his property and family and join the AIF as a fighting man. He did this in February last, and was passed as first-class by the doctor. For a time he was trained in the Artillery, and then suddenly was drafted into the Labour Corps, the only reason given being that he was over age (39) – too old for a combatant unit. It would appear that the Federal authorities, having accepted this man as a volunteer, have now conscripted him as a labourer and are not making proper use of him. If his services are not required in the fighting force, surely it would be more advisable to allow him to go back to his property and produce wool, potatoes, maize, oats, and green feed, as he was doing before enlistment.

AUGUST NEWS ITEMS

The Government had earlier decided that **companies declaring dividends must not make payments exceeding 4 per cent**. Now, they realised that such an arrangement would be **hard to administer, and so they** withdrew this regulation. Whoops.

AJF, a Letter-writer, suggested that it should be noted that many government and other **buildings, including banks, and hotels, have rubber floors.** If there were taken up and replaced with other materials, hundreds of tons of rubber could be salvaged throughout Australia.

Many Letter-writers pointed out that with the ban on waistcoats, also called vests, men would suffer in winter from the cold. Indeed, it was several times suggested, **older men would contract illness such as colds and pneumonia, and might be at serious risk of their** lives.

The Directing Authority for Leather Supply said that, because of military need, it was **impossible to supply sufficient sole leather for civilian purposes**. Those civilians who might miss out on new shoes were advised to "make do". A spokesman pointed out that **wooden clogs**, if they were available, could be used in factories.

A man wrote "My **bootmaker** was patriotic enough to enlist, and because other bootmakers in town refuse to take new customers, and because all the shoes in my sizes are already sold, I will soon have nothing to wear on my feet. Could the kind spokesman **please tell me how I can "make do"?**

Barbers would no longer be allowed t**o open after noon on Saturdays**. This will make it difficult for factory and munitions workers to get their hair cut.

The US would soon be producing synthetic rubber.

The **US administration announced that** eight German men had earlier been landed in the US from a submarine, and had proceeded to attempt acts of sabotage. They had been caught, tried, and found guilty. **Six of them had now been executed via the electric chair,** and the two others each received sentences of over 30 years.

In France, **the Germans shot and killed 93 French Resistors.**

An **AIF Battalion returned to Sydney** today after a period of **three years** serving in **Libya, Greece, Crete and Syria.** They will have a brief leave and then join our Forces in the defence of Australia. The Battalion cannot be named for "security reasons", and the censors seem certain that the thousands of family who met them will not divulge this information.

Australian Catholics will be allowed to **eat meat on Fridays** for the duration of the War. This is because of a temporary shortage of accommodation in Hell, caused by the heavy War demand. It is not clear **whether enemy aliens**, with their dubious status, are exempt.

The Australian Red Cross had arranged for **6,000 parcels of comforts to be distributed to Australia's POWs** in European camps at Christmas.

EUROPEAN EVENTS

Russia was fighting losing battles on all three fronts. Slowly, ever so slowly, a few miles a day, they were being pushed back. These were not routs by any means. They were hanging in there, waiting and hoping that Hitler would run out of steam. But the cost in man-power, to both sides, was beyond belief, so that it was certain that the ultimate winner would surely be a loser.

Britain was still beset by the submarines along her trade routes. Over the last few months, many sinkings had occurred just off the coast of America.

In Egypt, all was quiet after the previous frantic month. But no one should be fooled. Both sides were re-enforcing, and readying for a big battle soon.

A curious episode was acted out in coastal France. The Allies launched a raid on territory round Dieppe, not well known for anything. They gained a beach-head, and landed a goodly (censored) number of troops, and shot up a few miles of land for a few days, and then retired back to England. Why they did this was anyone's guess. Was it a rehearsal for a bigger invasion soon to come? Was it an attempt to pacify Russian demands for a Second front? Was it just an extra brandy late at night for a strategist? No one had the faintest idea. Curious.

AUSTRALIAN EVENTS

Japan continued bombing our north-most cities, and we kept bombing the townships they had occupied. We were breaking perhaps a little better than square.

The Americans invaded the Solomons. These were a series of islands to the north-east of Australia, and were significant only because the Japs had taken them. So the Yanks wanted them back. Over the course of the month, it appeared that the Americans were being successful on most of the islands, but the information we got was so restricted, and so heavily censored, that it was impossible to say what was going on. It seemed we should be pleased, but it could all be made in Hollywood as far as the average Oz citizen was concerned. We would have to wait.

The same was true for the Kokoda Trail. We all knew that the Japs had landed about 5,000 troops on the north of New Guinea. Or was that 10,000 troops? In any case, we were getting a few reports that the Japs had moved south to Kokoda, and were holding firm there. We later got reports that they were now in retreat. Or, were they back again? Again, the censor was the hardest worked man in the nation, and he was giving nothing away. As one correspondent said "how can this nation blindly give support to an Army that won't tell what is happening. We can take the bad news, but if we know nothing, then we can't support what we know nothing about". Alas, this was the case, and the citizens back home scarcely had any knowledge at this stage of the truly heroic deeds of our fighting sons.

CURTIN'S TOUGH MONTH

Prime Minister John Curtin found August a tough month. He had a number of messages from his powerful friends overseas that suggested he was a pain in the neck. He still wanted Britain and America to send more aid, other than words, to Australia. For Britain, he wanted Churchill to send our remaining troops back home from British control. Perhaps a few British aircraft or ships might be helpful. For America, he noted that the number of American troops in the region was only 20 per cent of the Oz force. He appreciated that **the US had no actual commitment to send any troops** at all, but he argued it was in **our mutual interest** to increase the flow as quickly as possible.

Roosevelt responded to Curtin's August pleas with the go-away statement that extra forces were being considered. He added some numbers that pretended to show that we had sufficient forces here to repel boarders. Churchill replied, again, that the war in Europe was the Number One priority of the Allies, and Australia would get its turn **in due course**.

McArthur made it clear that the US forces here were in fact here only **because he regarded Australia as a base from which to attack the Japanese in the Pacific. But not because of any plan to protect Australia.** It was just a means to an end. While it can be argued that each of these responses had its own logic, Curtin saw it from an Australian point of view, and worried and worried that the invasion of Australia was imminent.

His state of near-depression was exacerbated by Billy Hughes. William Morris Hughes had been in Australian politics since before Federation, he had been Prime Minister, he was now the Leader of the Opposition UAP, was quite a firebrand, and also quite a political opportunist. In August, he complained that some material that had been published in British papers had been censored as it left that country, and that the heavy hand of the Censor was depriving Oz of the news it coveted. "The Little Digger's" claim was unanswerable, and the nation cheered his remarks.

Rattled, Curtin sprang to the defence of his Ministers and, in doing that, he uttered some statements that rankled with the public. He warned that unless we developed greater cohesion and supported the war effort more, he would introduce Acts that would "reduce us down to subsistence level". This irritated people because the vast majority, either in the Services, or the factories or elsewhere, were already doing everything the Government specified. If they were not doing more, it was because of **the Government's lack of direction, ineptitude, and bungling that was muddying everything.**

He also said that the administration provided by the Government was the best that it was possible to produce. This was clearly wrong. Admin in general across all aspects of the war economy was nowhere near up to scratch. And at the level of Parliament, it was clear that **there were better men than the current incumbents** ready to take their place in office, given a chance. Most people thought that an all-party Government would improve admin greatly.

It ended up a bad month for Curtin, but despite severe criticism of him, **he maintained his personal popularity**. His basic honesty and sincerity, his capacity for hard work, and his intelligence all combined to get him through with the populace. A man as sensible and sensitive as Curtin could scarcely shrug off such a month, but like the realist he was, he was ready at the start of September to keep grinding away at the measures he felt important. Despite his small blemishes, he was truly a great leader.

TWO LETTERS ON POLITICS IN OZ

Many Letters were published this month dealing with the issues raise above, and related matters. I have select two of the moderate ones that reflect the majority views.

Letters, Geoffrey Fenton, Member of the Council of the National Defence League, Sydney. Should war or politics be the paramount consideration now? Surely there can be only one answer to that. And yet, at a moment like this, when, as Sir Earle Page says, "the danger to Australia is still very great and very close," when the whole war situation is balanced on a knife-edge, on one side of which are possibilities of disaster almost too horrible to contemplate, we have this sorry spectacle of political bickering.

It is within my knowledge that men of the AIF who have returned to Australia after two and a half years of bitter warfare, during which they risked everything for the land and the cause they hold dearer than life, have been shocked to find in their homeland such an atmosphere. If the censorship has faults, amend them; if the War Council needs strengthening, strengthen it; if any wholehearted patriotic thing needs to be done, do it. But, in the name of sanity, in the name of common decency, let us act as one, resolute Australian people. Is it too much to hope for a united Government composed of the best elements of all parties?

Whether we agree entirely or not with Pope that "Party is the madness of many for the gain of a few," it must be abundantly clear to every sane person that the resurgence of the party spirit at this time of imminent peril to our country and our Empire is unworthy of this stalwart nation.

Letters, Aussie and Ex-Digger 1914-18, Sydney. Apart from any personal political views, I think it will be generally conceded that Mr Curtin and his Ministers have made a most creditable attempt at doing a good job of work. Why then all this sniping and sharpshooting from the Opposition? It appears to be a systematic attempt to embarrass the Government. If we make a successful stand, finally best our enemies, and thus retain our freedom, it will be time enough then to have a political, economic, and social spring-cleaning. Till then, we have to accept and endure many things we dislike and probably resent.

Instead of indulging in so much carping criticism, let us try and realise what a colossal job our leaders have on their hands; the tremendous mental strain it involves and constant drain on physical resources. Theirs is an almost superhuman task. To put it in the words of the average Australian, "what about giving them a fair go?"

TROUBLES IN NEW GUINEA

There was no doubt that our soldiers involved in fighting were doing as good a job as anyone could want. But there were others aspects of living with the military, interacting with the community, that deserve a look.

When the Japs started to invade through Papua, the last of the Oz inhabitants were forced to evacuate. This meant they had to leave their homes at short notice, and they were assured that the Army would care-take their homes.

As it turned out, their homes were looted. Sadly, it was Australian Army soldiers who did the looting.

Letters, Papuan. As one of those unfortunates who have suffered very severely from the looting which took place at Port Moresby, I feel that if the true facts which led up to the ransacking of homes and private property generally were made known, either the Department of the Army or the War Damage Commission would be authorised to compensate the European population.

When it is remembered that all males under the age of 45 years were called up for military service at two hours notice, and thus had no opportunity of even locking up their homes, also that most of the males over 45 years were told to leave Port Moresby at 48 hours notice, so that the Army would have full charge of the town, surely those persons who left their homes and belongings in the care of the Army should be compensated for what has been taken. How are the people of Papua again to make a start in that difficult country unless at least their homes and the contents of same are restored to them?

Letters, L Tracey. I spent 18 years in Papua, and on February 18 I was compulsorily evacuated from the country by the Army, and was forced to leave all my possessions behind. Since leaving I have been informed that all my personal belongings have been taken by the Army. My home and furniture are all gone. Surely the War Damage Insurance scheme should cover this loss.

RUFFIANS IN UNIFORM

Letters, W B.   At 7 o'clock on Monday evening, whilst waiting at the corner of Sydney's Pitt and Market Streets for a tram to the railway, I was accosted by a young, big husky in uniform, who claimed me as a returned Digger. (I have served in both wars and was wearing my League badge.) After the usual preliminaries, he asked for money for himself and his mate, I refused and walked away, but he followed me and abused me, and made a swing at me. I closed with him to try and protect myself, but, as I am approaching 60, and am pretty sick, I had no chance.

He attacked me unmercifully three or four times, but I could only cover up and try to save my face and eyes. There were plenty of people around, including Navy and Army men, but no one came to my assistance, and I got a bad mauling. I was completely bewildered by the whole occurrence, but ultimately managed to stagger on to a tram and get away.

There were, of course, no police about, and it is for that reason I wish to draw public attention to this menace to our civic life. It is time that these ruffians, masquerading in khaki, were drastically dealt with. My only son has been missing since Malaya, and it is due to the memory of the real men of the AIF, who have sacrificed and suffered, that we should make it our business to exterminate the parasites who would, if unchecked, make the name of the 2nd AIF infamous.

The attack on me was so vicious, so uncalled for, and so unmerciful, that if I had had a gun in my pocket I would have used it without hesitation. Failing a gun, I intend for the future to carry a short iron bar about with me at night.

Letters, J F Moseley. Oscar Wilde used to say that nature follows art, and there is something in this contention. It may be said, for instance, that Victorian novelists **created** just as much as they portrayed the Victorian Englishman. **Australian writers are now moulding Australian character** in the say way and on none of us is the effect so noticeable as on soldiers in uniform. These are mostly young fellows with practically unformed characters, so they live the part written for them. The part is that of an uncouth tough ignorant of all rules of social behaviour. The "Ginger Mick" tradition has been carried on to such lengths that the suggestible bulk of the army think that all Australian must be "blokes and coves and coots" and that **false** picture of Australians has travelled abroad.

American writers have built up a different legend around their soldiers: in their literature and journalism **the Doughboy is a clean, smart, keen, chivalrous chap** with great respect for himself, who always does the right thing. It seems that the Doughboys try to live this part, just as our chaps seem to feel **obliged to live the sillier part laid down for them by Australian writers.** War itself is brutalising enough in all conscience, but there is no need to aggravate its effects on personality.

Cannot our writers build up a different and better part for our soldiers to live?

Comment. Servicemen on week-end leave were a real menace round city pubs. There were always tons of drunks around, and they were certain to break out in brawls at various times as closing time grew near. Civilians were generally not involved unless they wanted to be. With the advent of the Americans on to the scene, these brawls took on an international flavor. Every Monday, there were Court Reports in the Papers of soldiers who had mis-behaved badly enough to end up in Police custody at the week-end. The hospitals did a roaring trade as well.

MILITARY POLICE

These gentlemen had a reputation of not being at all gentle. One of their duties was to keep the Saturday-night drinkers out of trouble, and they did this by riding round the cities in vans, and arresting drunken and brawling young men. The idea was somehow to get them back to base and have them dealt with by military discipline. By this stage of the War, business was brisk for the MPs, and their jobs seemed secure.

MPs were also used to find **military deserters**. Most of these were young men who went on leave and did not return to base on time. Some of them were too drunk to make it, others felt that a two-night dalliance with a young girl was the love of their life. Generally these folk were easy to find, and were sent back to base where their wrists were slapped. Other serious deserters fled interstate, or hid with relatives, and ended up in the civil courts charged with desertion. This was a problem that had been faced by every Army that ever existed, and with only military figures to go on, it seems that this was a much smaller problem in the Australian Services than in most others.

CONSCIENTIOUS OBJECTORS.

These were men who, for one reason or another, claimed exemption from military service because it violated some personal principle that they held deeply. Most of the persons claiming exempt status were from religious backgrounds. Often these persons were prepared to serve overseas, but would not take up arms. Others would not go that far, and would not serve in the military at all, but were happy to serve in some type of civilian role that performed background work for the Forces.

Other applicants were not so genuine. They just wanted to get out of the military, and were prepared to feign all sorts of religious and humanitarian beliefs to avoid the realities of combat. It was the duty of the Civil Courts to hear the cases from different appellants, and there was a constant stream of young men coming before them.

"Conscies", once accepted as such by the Courts, were not popular in Australia. This was a world where men were being slaughtered overseas every day, and where death lists appeared every morning at the breakfast table. Healthy young men everywhere, not in uniform, were constantly scowled at by others for not "being in there", and to try to explain your decision as being one of the conscience was near impossible. The Government's position changed back and forth as the years of war went on, but it seemed that gradually the conscies were accepted as being part of the landscape, an inevitable consequence of war, but the **individuals** were **never** accepted as the honest decent citizens that many of them doubtless were.

A FEW COMMENTS

Letters, Daisy Bates. I greatly regret the rationing of tea, which, to my mind, has been the foundation beverage of Australia's best pioneers. I have drunk tea for over 60 years, and in those 30 odd years of my camp-life amongst the natives – wild and semi-civilised – their first drink of a pannikin of sweetened tea was a revelation to them, and its energetic effect was at first supposed to be due to my "magic." When they would return from a long bush walk, "tea, gul-dhar, kabbarli" (tea, grandmother), was their first cry.

In the early days of squatting tea was the uniform "pick-me-up" at "smoke-ohs" in shearing shed and cattle camp. Many like myself must miss the energising cup of tea that came so refreshing in cold or heat. My energy never flagged in all my years of work, while I could have my cup of tea at the end of the day's work. I have no substitute for it.

SEPTEMBER NEWS ITEMS

Tokyo authorities advised that **1800 civilian**s, some Australians, **would sail from Tokyo today**. These are not POWs, rather they were persons who were in Japan when war was declared. A similar number of Japanese nationals will sail simultaneously for Japan.

A new **entertainment tax** will be paid from today. It applies to all venues that provide entertainment, including all forms of theatre and sports events. Churches are not included. The cost of a visit to the pictures, that previously cost one Shilling, will now cost one Shilling and threepence. That is a 25 per cent increase.

The black market in clothing and petrol had grown in the last month. Drastic penalties involving years in prison will be imposed in future.

There were a lot of written and spoken comments about **compulsory unionism. Supporters of the idea** argued that the Unions had clubbed together and forced many gains from employers. **Non-unionists were free-loading**, and were not contributing to the costs involved in doing this....

Opponents argued that it was against the understood national code of free association. Also that much of **Union funds went to the Labour Part**y, and they did not support that. Further, that many **Union officials were rogues and stand-over men** who abused their position.

The matter of **compulsory unionism simmered for months**. In fact, ten years later it was passed into law in NSW, but was never enforced.

Women's groups were constantly working to collect money for Comforts Funds for the Services. They had been **sending tobacco products to soldiers at the battle front**, but a recent Ruling by the Customs Department said it must **continue to pay Duty on the products**. The women had been hoping that the goods would become **duty-free**. This was especially so because the same goods were very much cheaper in US canteens just a few yards away - but only for US military.

The King had called for a day of prayer to mark **the third anniversary, on September 3rd, of Britain's declaration of war**. Churches in Australia were filled to overflowing, even though this was a normal Thursday.

September 5th. An **un-named** Oz freighter was sunk **a few months** ago off the Australian coast. Five men were killed. Questions were raised as to what could be gained by not supplying the name of the freighter, and by delaying the news for "a few months". After all it was argued, **the Japs would already have all that information and more. Why the schoolboy secrecy?**

Management in a number of munitions factories have decided that **Sunday night shifts should be abandoned**. This was because of the high degree of absenteeism for that shift. One-third of the workers were not turning up for work. One manager said "the poor buggers are too tired to keep it up."

MILITARY NEWS

At the end of September, things seemed a little better on a number of fronts. In New Guinea, Australian forces had thwarted **a Japanese invasion at Milne** Bay, on the very east of New Guinea. **On the Kokoda Track**, the Japs appeared to have run out of steam and everything else, like food and ammunition, that they needed to keep advancing. They appeared to be withdrawing, though no one was all that certain. **In the Solomons**, the Americans were slowly consolidating, and had withstood a major counter-attack. In all three battle areas, **the Japanese Army had tried, and failed. Perhaps they were not invincible, after all. Fingers crossed.**

The Brits in Egypt were waiting for the Germans to make an all-out attack. The Germans were getting in re-inforcements. So the month passed relatively quietly, with the Brits appearing to get the better on any encounters that did happen.

MORE FINGERS CROSSED

In Russia, the Germans pushed forward on all fronts and made small murderous gains for most of the month. At the end of the month, **those advances all seemed to come to a halt.** Particularly at Stalingrad, where the Germans **actually had conquered a number of suburbs**, the resistance started to fight back. **Maybe**, the Germans had stretched themselves too far, and maybe they were being held in positions where they could not get the assistance they were desperately needing. **Maybe. Who knows? This time, cross your toes as well.**

Comment. Most of our Army on the Kokoda Trail was made up of reservists. These were young men who had volunteered or were conscripted on the understanding that they would not have to serve overseas. As it turned out, New Guinea was classified as **Oz territory**, and so these reservists were quietly sent there.

Compared to the Japanese, they were complete amateur soldiers. These lads had no battle experience, and only about three months training. The Japanese Army, on the other hand, had been fighting in China since 1937, so many of them were hardened soldiers. **The average age of our soldiers was less than 19 years**, so it is indeed appropriate to call them "our **boys**."

CROONING AND JAZZ

Every now and then, a correspondent sends in a Letter to the Papers that, despite the fact that it is silly and irrelevant, sparks off a chain of equally-silly responses that end up quite entertaining. This year, in 1942, such Letters and chains, had been noticeably absent until now. But here, at last we have a good number of frivolous Letters to ponder on. **Maybe, just maybe, it is a sign** that the mood of the people is lightening up a bit, and their fears of invasion have diminished.

Letters, Handel. May I protest against the frightful emanations that devastate the atmosphere at all hours of the day through our radio sets? Particularly violent are the early morning sessions. Jazz bands, with saxophonic screeches and gurgles, are violent in their discord, suggest an inferno in a low-down night club, and we are given love-sick crooners –

male and female – wailing tenors and baritones, whose vocal efforts can be surpassed by many contributors at a local "smoko."

In this city we have a Conservatorium of Music and musical competitions organised for the purpose of educating the public to a taste for decent music. In addition, there are musical societies whose performances are a delight to listen to. Yet all this talent is subordinated to imported rubbish that reeks with vulgarity and degeneracy. We have a censorship on literature and films mainly for their immoral influence. There is such a thing as immorality in music: why not stifle it now and let us have something that does not savour of indecency and "sloppy" sentiment.

Letters, K M. "Handel" should give his set to some soldiers' **Comforts fun**d, and get his future entertainment from the nearest cemetery. The reason for the popularity of the type of music to which he objects is the fact that, unlike "decent music," no societies or conservatoriums are needed to educate the common herd to enable them to understand it. Moreover, the sentiment of the modern fox trot or waltz tune, which "Handel" finds so degenerating, is exactly that which has been the theme of all popular music for the last 200 years. You don't have to take it seriously. What else can you write a song about, after all?

What is there objectionable in it? Admittedly, some of the modern jitterbug dancing looks unsavoury, but you can't blame the music for the way people interpret it. Modern music has a definite place in the modern world. It is used in factories to break the monotony and increase production through the psychological uplift it gives the workers. Classical music is no use there.

Letters, John Steel. "Handel of Deewhy" hits the nail on the head. The modern so-called music of America is turning nations crazy.

We in Australia should not only boycott the affliction, but request our Government to outlaw the fiendish ebullition of these sound-crazy hoodoo-ites of Hollywood.

I urge the collocation and playing of continental (European) bands and other music, also the collocation of real Chinese and Indian music – the sweet cadences of which, when heard, will be remembered for many a day. We should cultivate and perpetuate our own Australian music, original and of the soil – racy. About 50 per cent of the so-called classical music is utter rubbish, though not as bad as jazz and crooning. It is often meaningless and destitute of harmony. Vienna waltzes and Stephen Foster's melodies are replete with melody. Melody, cadences, harmonies, and above all simplicity, are real music. Folk and ballad music, village choir singing, even the Pacific Islands songs, are replete with melody. We should have more of them.

Banish jazz and crooning, by law, if necessary, but banish them.

Letters, F A R. "Handel's" objection to jazz is pointless, in that it is based on a comparison of two things which have widely different functions. In common with many others, he condemns jazz because he cannot find in it the aesthetic appeal found in classical music. The main function of jazz is not to give aesthetic satisfaction, but to make people dance. An analogy to his argument would be the contention that a Bateman cartoon was worthless because it did not have the aesthetic appeal of a Rembrandt portrait.

Perhaps if "Handel" were to listen to some jazz without the prejudice which seems to be shown in his choice of words, he might appreciate something of its ingenious orchestration, cunning rhythms, and technique of improvisation, and realise that an appreciation of Beethoven and Duke Ellington is neither inconsistent nor impossible.

Letters, Cecilia. While at home doing various tasks, I often long for an hour or two of music while I work. I turn on the wireless – a fearful nasal voice is wailing a sloppy love song. I turn to another station, and am greeted with loud noises and screeches. I go slowly round the dial and strike a jazz band. Then I switch off.

Possibly a lot of young – and even old – people are thrilled with delight at these programmes; but surely one out of all the stations we have might cater for the music-loving minority. I used to be surprised to hear educated and musical people say they hated a wireless! Now I realise they were forced to listen to their friends and neighbours' wireless wailings and judged accordingly.

Letters, H Cotter. From various opinions expressed by your correspondents, it would appear that the modern swing music of today is in keeping with the spirit of the age. This finds expression in the restless semi-barbaric music which has its origin in the jungles of West Africa, and has found an outlet among the negroes of the United States, by whom it has been popularised.

It is said that when a gramophone record of swing music was played before some placid introspective North American Redskins, they expressed high displeasure by means of grunts and signs. On the other hand, on hearing a classical record, they were lulled into a state of ecstacy. How true the old saying, "That music hath charms to soothe the savage breast." Does modern swing music fall into this category? I wonder.

HANDEL who started this correspondence, now returned to have the last say.

Letters, Handel. F A R states that the function of jazz music was to make people dance: I would like to inform him that a similar effect can be produced, with a less excruciating method, by hitting one's thumbnail with a hammer.

SMOKING IN TRAMS.

Letters, John Perry. I notice that there is to be **no distinction** between smoking and non-smoking compartments in trams and buses **between certain hours of the night and early morning.** Why cannot this distinction be cut out altogether? It was introduced in the early part of the century to protect the ultra-sensitive nostrils of the **dainty ladies** of the period from the annoying fumes.

Nowadays, one sees members of the opposite sex of all ages and descriptions smoking, not only in public conveyances, but even on the streets, and another male prerogative has disappeared for ever. The trams and buses are so packed with people that the unfortunate conductors have quite enough to do in collecting fares without looking for people who may have the temerity to offend the susceptibilities of some sensitive persons by smoking in a so-called non-smoking compartment. In any event, tobacco has become so scarce and the price so prohibitive that we will soon see communal pipes, as in Eastern countries.

Letters, Livingstone Mote. At last we know from the letter of John Perry on this subject what is wrong with Australia: we have been too considerate to those with finer feelings. No doubt Mr Perry has long ago flung away any traits belonging to the early part of the century, such as thoughtfulness for others, respect for the rights of others, and the observance of public regulations. We should by now prove ourselves modern. If he could be accepted as the leader of Australia, Mr Perry would doubtless proclaim the slogan, "Away with sensibility; be strong; at all times and in all places pour forth smoke, in your neighbour's face, over his clothes, on his food; revel in noise of yelping dogs, of blaring radios, of loud conversation – in a word be a man; consider yourself and nobody but yourself; follow me; Advance Australia Fair."

COMMENT ON "SPORTS"

Letters, F Carlile. It is high time that horse racing and uncommercialised competitive games ceased to be referred to under the one collective term "sport." Whereas the nation at war can unquestionably curtail horse racing, we cannot afford to take from our youth the stimulus to healthy development given by such competitive games as football, athletics, and swimming. Surely it is the duty of the Government, rather than to curtail sport in which youth is an active participant, to stimulate these games which are the backbone of a vigorous nation.

WASTEFUL CROCKERY LOSES WARS

Letters, M L. While making a purchase I heard the following dialogue: "I'll take the coffee set, five Pounds 15 shillings, and lay-by the teaset, six Pounds 10 shillings. If we can't spend what we like on clothes, we can on things for the flat. I don't really need the tea-set , but I may as well have it while I can." There are hundreds of women doing more than their bit, but there are many playing into enemy hands by willful waste.

ECONOMIC MATTERS, PERSONAL FINANCE.

Letters, A J P. As a poor and aged man with a very small income, which has been considerably reduced by the reduction of interest rates, I feel that the Prime Minister's appeal for austerity in our living would have much greater effect if he were to give a lead by reducing the salaries of our Federal members. Such a step would show that the Government was sincere in its appeal to us poor people.

Letters, Compulsory. There seems to be growing recognition of the fact that to rely on voluntary contributions to supply the financial needs of the war amounts to a shirking of responsibility. "Compulsory" is admittedly a word that falls harshly upon democratic ears, but we accept compulsion every day without complaint when we obey a traffic signal, keep to the left side of the street, and do or refrain from doing a score of other things that are restricted by laws or regulations. Recognising that these restrictions are for the common good, we accept them and obey them automatically.

Surely there can be no argument as to whether **compulsory war saving** is for the common good. It is more than that; it is vital to the preservation of our national existence. Can any average person honestly say that to save 3/- a week would be a burden? If it were taken from him at the source he would soon forget that it had gone. But if he thought about it at all, he would have the satisfaction of knowing that it was helping to keep the flag flying and was only a loan, anyway.

Letters, A Lottery Subscriber. I think the Government is missing an opportunity of raising a large sum annually. The majority of subscribers to lotteries, I feel certain, would not object to a tax of, say 3d or 6d on each 5/- ticket, and the said tax could be collected without cost. It could be called a war tax, and the name should be the "Austerity

War Tax" and could go on indefinitely until the end of the war.

Letters, Barton Addison. The Prime Minister has shown that the peril in which Australia stands makes it imperative to end all superfluous activities. He warns us that essential industries must suffer curtailment – so urgent is the national demand for man-power. The public is awake to the necessity of severe rationing of many commodities, among which are newsprint and paper. Patriotic citizens are prepared to make necessary sacrifices for the preservation of their country.

In this State, as well as in others, lotteries still pursue their pre-war activities. In Sydney the State Lottery requires a large staff. It requires a large quantity of paper and printing and much space in the press for advertising results. Also many thousands of people daily throng the lottery office to buy tickets. In consequence, an already over-burdened transport system is called upon to carry extra traffic. Surely it will not be claimed that lotteries are an essential war service. Some people may claim that because net proceeds are distributed to the hospitals – that their continuance is essential. The answer to that is that such amount can be raised by a small direct tax at a smaller cost with the existing taxation organization – and resulting in saving man-power and material.

Under Mr Curtin's austerity campaign the State Lotteries might well be closed for the duration.

OCTOBER NEWS ITEMS

Letter from Observer, Waverley. The ordinary and accepted principles of British justice have been inverted in the campaign against black-marketing and profiteering. The **onus of proof there is on the accused to prove his innocence,** and not on his accusers to establish guilt.

News Item, Saturday, October 3rd. There will be no horse-racing today in **Australia**. Programmes will resume as normal next Saturday.

NES workers and wardens have had some concession from the Government. In future, workers injured on their way to or from work **will be eligible for compensation**.

Soldiers from New Guinea, now in hospital in Australia, say that, but for the almost **superhuman exertion of Papuan native**s, many wounded Australians would not have survived. They suggest that there **should be better recognition** of the natives' heroism than the **tins of bully beef** and the few shillings the soldiers could give them.

The Commonwealth Prices Commissioner told the Housewives Association that **it would be impossible to create an army of inspectors** to control chisellers and spielers **on the black markets**.

Price controls now apply to second-hand cars. For example, a car that is one-year-old must sell at or below 85 per cent of its initial cost. Three-year-old cars will sell at a discount of 35 per cent. These limits were set to prevent the price of old cars rising above the price of new ones **(which were virtually unobtainable)**.

NEWS FROM THE BATTLEFIELDS

October was another good month on all five fronts that concerned us. Not that we had terrific news. Rather, the news we got was never all that bad, and it was sometimes downright encouraging. It could always be checked by listening to Short Wave from Berlin and Tokyo, which were of course full of lies, but were pretty factual about advances and retreats.

So as best we could work out at the time, the Japs in **New Guinea** had slowly pushed forward along the track, through Kokoda, and finally reached a plateau from which they could just see Port Moresby. Their trip there had not been at all pleasant, because of the Australian opposition, and by the time they got there, they were exhausted, starved, and short of all supplies. **As was later reveale**d, on September 22nd, the military bosses decided at that stage to call it quits, and ordered the Jap troops back to the north coast. Some half of them were loaded onto ships, and away they went. The other half were spread out over the island, and were left as a rearguard, to fend for themselves.

From the Australian point of view, at that date, the enemy simply disappeared for the next ten days. Our troops proceeded with caution, fearing a trap, but they met only occasional opposition. For the rest of October, Australian troops played a cat-and-mouse game with the Jap rearguard, gradually beating them back further and further away from Port Moresby.

Back in Aust**ralia,** as far as we could tell, the threat to New Guinea **might** have gone, and one more sigh of **measured** relief was audible across the nation. But don't count on it.

In Guadalcanal, in the Solomons, US Forces were pitched in battle with the Japanese army and navy. In both cases, it seemed that the Japs were throwing everything they had at their enemy, but the US forces were holding out. Certainly, the news reports were encouraging, and if you subtracted about 50 cent, it seemed we were getting the better of it.

In Egypt, Montgomery was now in charge, and he was intent on not attacking the German lines until he had built up his forces enough to do the job. He had done this throughout August and September. But, by October 23rd, he was ready, so off he went. The Australians were at the forefront and even Churchill had to proclaim "The Australian 9th Division struck what history may proclaim as the decisive blow in the Battle of Alamein." This battle went on until November 6th, when the Allied Commander General Alexander cabled Churchill "Ring out the bells. The Eighth Army is advancing." Rommel was in full retreat, and he withdrew his forces 1,700 miles to the west. By then, the battles for Dunkirk, Libya, Egypt, and Alamein were over.

This last battle for Alamein was not without its costs. Australia lost 620 men killed, and 6,000 wounded. New Zealand lost another 6,000 killed and wounded. 20,000 Italian prisoners were taken, and 10,000 Germans. It was a wonderful, welcome victory for the Allies, and once again, a terrible calamity for the world.

Still, from Australia, the battle scene was the best it had been for months. But before we get too carried away with celebrations, we should wait a few more months, and see what this crazy yo-yo world has in store for us.

STATUTE OF WESTMINSTER

The British Parliament, in 1931, passed this legislation which, through a number of Clauses, acknowledged the rights of all Dominions **to make their own laws free from British interference**. In very broad terms, it said that the Dominions of the Empire could make their own laws if they chose, or they could continue to operate as before 1931 mainly from British law. And **then, from 1931**, if they did make new laws that were not consistent with British law, then those new laws would stand.

New Zealand and South Africa chose to ratify and implement the Statute immediately. Australia had not ratified it by 1942, but in that year, was planning to do so in October. The reason it had never been ratified was because **it represented a bond of kinship between the British and Australian**s, and because it maintained **the feeling in Australia** that we were part of an Empire, and as such, **that Britain would defend us with all its might if need b**e. It was a bit like the relationship we hope we have now with the US. We follow its foreign policy, readily maintain good genuinely-friendly relations, pee in its pocket, and hope they will help us out when we need help.

The immediate reason, for now denting the cozy relationship with the Brits, was that two Australian sailors had joined the Australian Navy, and transferred to the British Royal Navy. There, they committed a crime (censored) and were found guilty, and sentenced to death. Australia did not accept that this sentence should be carried out, and the only way to forestall this was to change certain legislation. That is, new legislation had to be brought down that differed from the British Clauses we had been using. To do that, **we needed to at last invoke the Statute of Westminster, and pass our own separate laws**.

BEHIND RATIFICATION OF THE STATUTE

The Labour Party, and its brains-trust of Curtin, Evatt and Chifley, had been battling for months to get more commitment from Britain to the defence of Oz. Churchill was always full of rhetoric that promised support for Australia in generalisations, but if you looked round our Oz cities on Friday nights, there were plenty of Yank servicemen on leave, but nary a Britisher. Lots of other things irked as well. Our Army's Ninth Division was still in Egypt, our best airmen were dropping bombs over Germany, not on the Japs. Our Sixth Division was still defending Ceylon, and not defending our shores. **The brains-trust wanted them all back in Australia.** There were other matters that rankled, especially in trade.

So they decided it was timely to ratify the Statute, and send the strong symbolic message that we were no longer wedded ever-so-firmly to the idea of Britain coming to our aid, but would make do without her. In fact, our efforts with the US were by now bearing fruit, military assistance was coming at a fair rate, and that assistance would continue as long as we were useful to the US cause.

It turned out that **the leaders of the Opposition**, Menzies, Hughes and Fadden, were also quite happy to have Australia break defence ties, and some other ties, with Britain at this time. So the Statute passed through both Houses with only a total of six Members dissenting.

Comment. The Statute signaled to everyone that **we were turning our face towards America**. There were very many people here who were complete Anglophiles and believed that Britain, and Churchill, could do no wrong. So it was politically important that **we did not at the same time appear to turn our back on Britain**. For once, our politicians did everything right, and the Statute was accepted with a minimum of fuss and to-do.

But, despite the low-key manner of its implementation, it was a matter of fundamental importance over the next three years of warfare. We had reached the stage where the **Brits were clearly not coming to our aid, and we needed to slowly, ever so slowly, get that message through to everyone in Australia.** The ratification of the Statute started that process of education.

RACING ON SATURDAYS

All through this year to date, there had been a very large number of Letters urging that all sorts of sporting activities should be stopped for the duration of the War. Mainly, there were few responses because most people thought that the writers were cranks of some sort, with a bee in their bonnets. But now that races had actually been stopped one Saturday each month, correspondents were eager to be heard.

Letters, W Cook. Time and time again we have been getting Letters in your columns from writers who want me to do what they say I should do. They want me to not drink beer, to not gamble, to not play sport, to go to Church, to work an extra 10 hours a week, and in my spare time do something to help the war effort. But these are the very same people who have been urging us all for ten years to become non-drinking, non-gambling, church-going goody-goodies.

Now they are nagging away again. But this time they cloak their mission in terms of the war effort. They ask how can we be on a race track enjoying ourselves if our young men are in the jungles fighting for our survival? How can we spend money on beer when our boys are sacrificing so much?

Let me tell you that if our fighting soldiers had a choice they would right now be on a race track drinking beer, and none of them would be in churches. If you asked them what they wanted for **us** in our short leisure time, they would say we should go drink beer at the races.

Have you noticed how all the wowsers always end their Letters. At the end, they add a final paragraph to add the sanctity of Christendom to their orders for us. Something like "with the grace of God we will come through this man-made crisis, but only if we turn to God and give up our wicked ways." What an argument they present. A combination of patriotism, and God, and survival. What a pity for them when the War is over, and they lose their patriotism and survival planks.

Letters, RACEGOER. I think we should re-think the bans on racing if we base the objection on economic grounds. When you have a bet, and lose, it goes to a bookie. But he has to pay out most of that money to other winners. In fact, the bookies keep only about 10 per cent of the money they handle. They keep about half of that for themselves, and the Government keeps the other half in taxes.

So betting results in the turnover of money, not in the destruction of wealth. The government gets more than its fair share. As well as that, society benefits because of the employment the industry provides, and I need hardly remind you that most racing workers are jockeys, ex-jockey trainers, or stable hands who are somewhat oversize jockeys. They are unsuitable for the Army or most other industries because they do not meet the stupid physical tests for height that are forced on them.

Further, the racing industry provides relaxation for hundreds of thousands of people across the nation. **No other single event does that.** We are a nation at this time that is working hard, possibly too hard. What is wrong with all those workers getting four hours recreation every week?

PETROL RATIONING AND EMPTY CARS

Petrol rationing for Oz had been introduced over a year ago. At the moment, **private motorists had been reduced to a monthly ration that only gave them a quick glimpse of the road each week**. As a consequence, about one quarter of motorists had moved their car to the back of the garage, and put it up on chocks to save the tyres, and then **sold their ration tickets on the black marke**t. Most of them decided that they should have two or three short trips per month, perhaps to church on Sundays, or to the golf course at the weekend.

There were other users who got larger allowances. For example, **doctors, who in those days made home visits**, got more. So too did trades-people. Also, businessmen for their many treks to offices and their various appointments.

The not surprising result of all this was that the number of cars on the roads, going to the city on a weekday, was greatly reduced. Many of them carried one solitary businessman. At the same time, buses and trams were crowded. The Letters below sprang from this situation.

Letters, James E Cornell. Cecile Hunter expects motorists with empty cars to give people a lift into town, but is she aware that by doing this the motorist is incurring a heavy financial liability in case he should have an accident and injure his passenger?

Letters, Unselfish. We read criticism of motorists driving empty cars. I am one of them, but usually have goods aboard for delivery. Apart from responsibility in case of accident, one may not be going the same way, and cannot spare time or petrol to suit strangers. As regards women waiting for trams, they will not ride in strange men's cars. I have offered and been snubbed, so ought to know.

Letters, Cecile Hunter. I wonder does "James Cornell" know that in London, since the war, car owners chalked their destination on the windscreens of their drive, and anyone was at liberty to hail them and to ask for a lift. I suppose this was their idea of good citizenship in war time. I do not know whether their insurance policies covered the accidents referred to by Mr Cornell, or if they did not have time to worry about remote possibilities, probably the latter.

Letters, James E Connell. In reply to "Cecile Hunter," I should say that, firstly, one can – without incurring financial responsibility in case of injury or death to a passenger – give a lift to anyone provided that the passenger agrees to accept all responsibility, but it seems to me to be against human nature for anyone injured to remember it was so agreed. It is unlikely that the executors of the deceased's estate would accept the driver's word for it. Perhaps the reason why the notice on cars in London is so prominently displayed is that it is to be taken as evidence that the passenger accepts the responsibility.

Letters, W E Hart. In this matter one vital and interesting point seems to have been overlooked. If an owner of a private vehicle drives a person to his destination, when a tram, bus, or train is available, notwithstanding the fact that this transport may have been complimentary, the owner commits a breach of the transport regulations, as he thus causes a loss to the Government of anticipated revenue and renders himself liable to prosecution.

Comment. This series of Letters is another example of a topic, hardly worth worrying about, growing legs, and grabbing its own audience. I repeat that such a sequence did not occur a few months ago, and the return of such silliness was a welcome sign for the nation.

I add that it might seem silly to suggest that inspectors would nab people for offering rides to others. But at the time, officialdom and inspectors were checking and enforcing everything. No one would have been surprised to see the prosecutions that Mr Hart rightly or wrongly anticipated.

FOOD AND DIET

Letters, Margaret McLoughlin. The inclusion of canned orange juice in the diet of soldiers is pandering to their taste, rather than supplying the vitamins necessary to their health, since already they have first preference of the foods abundant in these essential vitamins. Surely it is not a question of sacrifice for them to leave the oranges to the babies of this country.

Moreover, the supply that is made available to the public will be quickly snapped up by those best able to afford the price – people without children, and with a lifetime of the right food to sustain them. Adults can well carry on; it is our babies who will bear the brunt. If the Allied soldiers must have their orange juice, the Government should introduce rationing, to ensure that the remaining supply goes to the army of babies,.

Comment. Mr Blake of Taree argued triumphantly in a long Letter that all the fuss about a shortage of prunes earlier this year had gone away. He says that prunes are no more valuable than any other fruit, and that mothers who cry out for them are reading too many womens' magazines.

Letters, G Tranter. The proposed health campaign can be made to serve both itself and the austerity campaign, if emphasis is laid upon the benefits which, in a large proportion of instances, would result from a change in our eating habits. We nearly all eat too much, and a decrease of about 20 per cent in Australia's food bill could probably be made with only good results.

Comment. What would Mr Tranter say now (in the 2020's) if he saw what the average Oz citizen ate now, and how big he has become?

Letters, C Gudgeon. The Government is endeavouring to dissuade people from unnecessary spending, so it should assist matters greatly were it to agree to allow those, who had a small area in their back gardens, **plant sufficient tobacco seedlings** for their own private use without compelling them to make a declaration as to the number of plants grown and forcing them to pay excise.

NOVEMBER NEWS ITEMS

NSW wants to reduce the brown-out. The Feds do not want to. Heffron, the NES Minister for NSW said today "we intend to fight incessantly for the relaxation of the intolerable darkness that hinders rather than helps the vigorous prosecution of the War. **The brown-out is the brain child of brass hats**, who have refused to admit the error of their ways."

Mr Jones of Mosman thinks that if the cities and municipalities paid **nine pence for a dead rat**, they would soon become scarce.

Saluting the colours. On Thursday there is to be a parade through Sydney of the Allied Navies and other forces. No doubt colours will be shown, and let us hope that the citizens of Sydney will **pay the compliment due the colours**. Servicemen will know, or they should know, that they salute the colours as they pass, but civilians may not know that **men remove their hats, and women bow.**

A prominent clergyman comments: The **two-up mania** grips its adherents to such an extent that they seem powerless to resist. One of the most common sights on a Friday night is the rush to the Pay Office, so as to commence the evil while the going is good. I have seen men lose their week's earnings in five minutes during these after-pay gatherings.

No interstate travel by rail will be permitted for **any purpose connected with the Melbourne Cup**.

PUFFING BILLY of Neutral Bay writes that a great deal of labour would accrue if **tobacco** for civilian consumption were manufactured and **sold only in plug form**. The amount of labour involved and the cost in cutting, packing, and printing in the marketing of tobacco in its present form must be enormous.

FED-UP wants public phones to go dead after three minutes. He won't have to wait for "**flapper gossips**" to finish.

The Federal Government will move **40,000 workers from shops to the War industry**, including the armed services. **Most of them will be taken from big city store**s, so that "any fall in turnover will not cause an increase in prices."

PENSIONER of North Sydney thinks one of the greates**t curses about drinking is** the playing of dominoes in hotels. "I know of men who so spend most of their time when working, and a lot of old-age pensioners, my husband being one of them".

The Minister for Misery, Mr Dedman, has placed **a complete ban** on commercial **advertising promoting sales of goods or gifts over Christmas, New Year, or Easter**. He did not include any reasons for his decision....

Two days later, the Secretary of the Retail Traders Association, in a letter of protest described Mr Dedman as "**the man who killed Santa Claus.**"

FROM THE BATTLEFIELDS

As it turned out, it was indeed too early to celebrate victory in **New Guinea**. In early November, Australian and US troops found 14 miles of deep defences manned by 9,000 Jap soldiers in the northern region of Buna and Gona. In often hand-to-hand fighting, it took our troops almost three months to rout and clear out these determined and fanatical patriots, who fought-on, knowing their chances of either victory or escape had all gone. The final battle for New Guinea took place on January 22nd 1943 at Sanananda Point, where "a group of 100 Japanese, nearly all sick and wounded, refused demands to surrender, and were killed to a man."

The New Guinea campaign took 2,165 Australian lives, and 671 Americans. Also, malaria and fever incapacitated 40,000 Aussies troops. But **this** time, it **was** all over. The immediate threat to Australia had moved far from our shores, and perhaps soon the lights could go on again.

NORTH-WEST AFRICA

First, a little mix of geography, logistics and military strategy. Across the north of Africa are five nations. Morocco, Algeria, and Tunisia were at this time still French colonies, and because France was occupied by the Germans, were subject to German say-so. Next was Libya, formerly Italian, but now on the verge of complete surrender to the Allied forces. And finally, there was Egypt that had been under British suzerainty for a long time.

All of these nations were in a great position to harass shipping in the Mediterranean, and also to launch air attacks on any part of southern Europe. For example, Italy, Greece, Yugoslavia, and even Germany. The Allies reasoned that the three remaining countries under French rule were worth capturing.

So, on November 8th, British and American troops, under the supreme command of Dwight Eisenhower, landed in north-west Africa at Casablanca in Morocco, and at six places in Algeria.

By November 11th, all resistance was halted, but not before 3,000 troops had been killed on each side.

Only Tunisia remained. That becomes part of next year's story, but, in brief, the Germans and French put up a good fight under Rommel again, for a few months. Thereafter, theirs' was a losing battle that ended in mid-May. At that point, all of North Africa was under Allied control, and "the soft under-belly of Hitler's empire" was exposed.

Comment. As an interesting aside, let me add that on November 11th, the Germans formally occupied **the southern half of France**, where the French Vichy government had been acting under the fiction of autonomy. Then, two weeks later, **the Germans were worried** that the remaining half of the French fleet at Toulon might break out from that harbour, and go to the aid of the Allies in north Africa. With that in mind, **they scuttled all the remaining French fleet where it was anchored**. Three battleships, eight cruisers, seventeen destroyers, sixteen subs, and seventy other vessels went to the bottom. France now had fully lost its fleet, its armies, its colonies and its freedom.

A NATIONAL GOVERNMENT - AGAIN

At least half the population had been crying out all year that this nation needed a National Government, such as Britain had put together, for the War years. They wanted a Cabinet of about 16 elected Parliamentarians, **coming from both sides of politics, who would hold all Ministerial position**s. That would mean that Mr Curtin would still be Prime Minister, but that about half his Cabinet would come from the UAP and Country Party.

It was argued that at the moment there were many potential Ministers in the latter two Parties who would be better than the current ones. Also, that, if the new Cabinet made decisions together, then they would be accepted by all Parties, and the silly quibbling and back-stabbing would be done away with.

The gentleman below provides an interesting comment on this.

Letters, A Murray. I applaud, along with hundreds of others that I talk to in my barber shop, the ratification of the Statute of Westminster. Not that anyone wanted to break with Britain. It's just that our aims and needs are different from the old country, and we are best to decide what they are.

The aim of my Letter, is to point out that the ratification was done without any fuss because there was none of the normal "them" and "us" argument. It was as if we had a National Government, where after months of discussion, as there was, the Parties had quietly worked out what was best for Australia, and voted together for the approval.

Even such ratbags as Calwell, and Ward, found that they would be way out of court if they used it to grandstand on. For once, Evatt too avoided the heavy theatrics he normally employs, and steered the Bill through in a masterful fashion. **Its passage is as good an example of the workings of a National Government as you can get.**

THE POSTER-PROPAGANDA WAR IN BRITAIN.

Britain and the Allies, and the Axis, were deluging their own people and the enemy with messages that exhorted them to do something or other that would help their War effort. **Mostly they used posters at home, and increasingly they were dropping flyers on the enemy.**

The earliest posters in Britain came after the British fiascos in Norway and Dunkirk. As the realisation of the threats of Hitler's blitzkrieg sank in, propaganda stepped up, and Britain was flooded with visions of Hitler and his armies crushing foreign countries underfoot. The evil, helmeted German forces were depicted as bayoneting and garroting civilians, with their bombers dropping their loads on strong yeomen standing defiantly.

JAPANESE PROPAGANDA

A year later, we in Australia had caught up to the Brits in the propaganda war, and were pushing pretty much those same messages.

By the end of 1942, the Yanks were fighting side by side with our soldiers and airmen, and the Japanese sought to exploit the inevitable rivalry between the ground-forces in particular.

To do this, Jap planes dropped flyers on our troops in New Guinea. They aimed to sow dissatisfaction with the role America was playing in the War. The theme in the first was that the Yanks were taking it easy back in Oz, winning and violating the local girls, while Australian soldiers were losing their lives in New Guinea.

A second theme was once again that Oz soldiers were doing all the fighting, and that the US was getting ready to take over the nation and our resources.

Another form of Japanese propaganda was the broadcasting of radio messages, on Army frequencies or short waves, to the troops. **Announcer**s on these radio programmes were often natives of Allied countries. Charles Cousins, formerly of the Australian ABC, was one such. Equally famous was Tokyo Rose, a Japanese American initially from Hawaii.

Both of these, and others, kept up a flow of dispiriting and falsified news reports about the War, and for the Americans, little reminders of mum and apple pie, Christmas and Thanksgiving Day, and **the girlfriends who were in no way waiting for them**. It was all set in a framework of modernity with lots of jazz and crooning. No classical music here.

One particularly effective broadcaster was so-called Lord Haw-Haw, who broadcast each night for five years from Berlin. His calls were heard all over the world, including millions in Britain, and half a million in Australia. He gave daily descriptions of war events, suitably skewed to the hopelessness of the Allied cause, and pumped away at the folly of fighting on. By 1942 he was including the Pacific War, and Australia and New Guinea, in his pro-Axis commentary. Most people who listened came to treat him as a bit of a joke, and his name was uttered throughout this nation and elsewhere with contempt. But some of it stuck now and then, and it is generally agreed that his propaganda was the most effective of all.

William Joyce (Lord Haw-Haw), an American born of English parents, was captured at the end of the War and, as a British subject, he was tried for treason in 1946, and executed.

Comment. These propaganda efforts made little impact on citizens safe at home. But they did effect the men serving overseas. They undoubtedly had an impact on some men who could not work out why they were in New Guinea fighting for their lives, and not on the beach at Bondi. **For some, at home and abroad, the rate of desertions increased as the propaganda messages got through.**

DECEMBER NEWS ITEMS

Eight hundred Christmas parcels, packed by the Red Cross, will today be taken by trucks and planes to places where they will be distributed to **Papuan boys who worked as carriers and stretcher-bearers with the Oz Army**. They will contain matches, tobacco, cigarette papers, barley sugar, soap, and condensed milk.

The ban on the Communist Party, imposed two years ago, was lifted. This was hardly surprising, given the good conduct of local Reds so far in this War. Also, it should be remembered that two years ago, **Russia was a hated Communist power**, but that eighteen months ago she suddenly emerged as an ally, and had been fighting against Germany ever since.

Figures from Retail Traders across the nation indicated **that** sales this year were not affected by austerity measures and were holding at last year's levels.

From London: Britain's 1942 Christmas will be remembered for its **orgy of spending**, especially in London and the large provincial cities.

There would be **no fresh bread for four days** over the Christmas break in all major centres.

Sydney's **fourth** War-time **Christmas Day was spent quietly** in keeping with the Prime Minister's appeal for austerity. There were large congregations at city and suburban church services. Road traffic was the quietest for many years, though this could be put down to the absence of petrol.

On New Year's Eve, by order of the Production Executive of the Federal Cabinet, it was decreed that all parts of radio sets must be preserved for the Armed Forces. This will prevent **the manufacture of radio sets for civilians, and sales will cease as of now**.

Mr Dedman advised the public to "**go easy on matches**." He said that supplies will be adequate if economy is practiced by everyone.

Salt licks for sheep and cattle have been banned in NSW.

One opinion on Government policies. Mr John Macara, reflecting a growing opposition. "One hundred of Britain's leaders of industry this week said they adhered to their belief **in private enterprise, stimulated by the profit motive**. After **our bitter experiences of late, of bureaucratic control implemented by compulsion, many of us are ready to return to common sense**."

November 20. **David Jones's Market Street Store**, the famous Sydney landmark and major shopping outlet in Sydney, was **taken over by the Ministry of Munitions today**, and will be occupied shortly.

This war was really serious. I could give you a long list of lollies that cannot be sold. What is the point of **Saturday afternoon at the flickers** if you can't get your lollies? No bulls eyes, no musk sticks, no penny chocolates, no green frogs.... no nothing.

10 HIT SONGS FROM AMERICA

Deep in the Heart of Texas	**Bing Crosby**
Don't Sit under the Apple Tree	**Andrew Sisters**
Me and my Girl	**Judy Garland**
Walk Without You	**Harry James**
The Stagedoor Canteen	**Sammy Kaye**
My Devotion	**Vaughan Monroe**
Night and Day	**Frankie Lame**
Somebody Taking my Place	**Benny Goodman**
Sunshine of your Smile	**Bing Crosby**
White Christmas	**Bing Crosby**

A COMMENT ON OZ SONGS

There were very few new Australian songs in the market. There were some 78rpm battlers like **Road to Gundagai**, and **Pack up your Troubles,** but there was no sign of a vigorous industry as in America.

Peter Dawson was the Oz exception, with his rousing **On the Road to Mandalay**, but the big seller of non-US songs was Vera Lynne, who stole the air-waves with her plaintive **Blue Birds over the White Cliffs of Dover** and **We'll Meet Again.**

Some writers say she did more to win the War than Winston Churchill.

10 BIG MOVIES

Mrs Minerva	Greer Garson.
	Walter Pigeon
Random Harvest	Ronald Coleman
	Greer Garson
Road to Morocco	Bing Crosby
	Bob Hope
Casablanca	Ingrid Bergman
	Humphrey Bogart
Reap the Wild Wind	John Wayne
	Kirk Douglas
The Mummy's Tomb	Abbott, Costello
Moonlight Serenade	Betty Grable
	Victor Mature
Yankee Doodle Dandy	James Cagney
Gentleman Jim	Errol Flynn
This Gun for Hire	Alan Ladd

ACADEMY AWARDS

Best Actor: James Cagney (Yankee Doodle Dandy)

Best Actress: Greer Garson (Mrs Minerva)

Best Movie: Mrs Minerva

WAR NEWS

Surely, it was all too good to be true. Nothing was going wrong. Everything in fact, seemed to be going right. On every front, in Europe, in the Middle East, in the Pacific, in Burma, the Allies had hit the lead, were in front, were winning. This cannot be real. After all this time, it **has** to be a dream.

But a dream, it was not. In Russia, the Germans had taken a third of Stalingrad, but could go no further. Then the Russians quietly outflanked them, and all of a sudden, in December, 300,000 Germans were captured in one area. On other fronts, the Russian masses with their tanks fought yard-by-yard, and gradually got the upper hand. There was a long way to go, but all of a sudden everyone was talking about Napoleon's retreat from Moscow, and thinking that **history was about to repeat itself**.

Elsewhere, in the north of Africa, the clean-up from Egypt and Libya had gone well, and the fight for Tunisia could be held back until more resources were available. It was now only a matter of time. Africa was ours. So, that meant the Allies had air bases from which to attack Italy. Thus, places like Naples, Turin, and Milan were getting pasted night after night. Even the submarine war was turning our way. Everyone was now saying that we were destroying more subs than the Axis could produce, and that our losses of shipping were falling quickly.

That was in Europe. In the Pacific, our charmed life continued. In New Guinea, the Japanese had dug in round Buna and Gona on the North Coast. In December they were taking a lot of digging out, but our military infants were methodically, fox-hole by fox-hole, doing the job. In the Solomons the Yanks were gradually winning on land, sea, and air, and that threat had gone away.

People in Britain were in effect celebrating all this with their orgy of Christmas spending. Here in Oz, we were constantly being enjoined by Curtin, Dedman, Forde and others to take it easy, and to remember that there were years of trouble ahead of us before we could rest easily. But to a nation that six months ago was pretty sure that we would be conquered and invaded, the sudden release from **that** shadow was an enormous relief. Yet, it was all tinged with caution that centred on the certain knowledge that t**hose Casualty lists in the newspapers** would keep coming through, and that many thousands more of silly daring young and old men would be killed and maimed, and that the survivors would have to live with that. To the average householder, right across Australia, things were much better, indeed they were bright. If only our boys were all back, safe and sound in their own beds.

A FINAL COMMENT ON THE RUSSIAN WAR

Hitler made two enormous mistakes in his prosecution of the War. **Firstly, he invaded Russia in June 1941.** He had no need to do that. In fact, he was benefitting from the Treaties he already had with that nation, and could have comfortably gone on his merry way in the east, with Russia's implicit backing. But his philosophy, anti-Communist and anti-Jew, got the better of him, and he made his first great blunder.

His second error was to declare war on the US after she was attacked by Japan at Pearl Harbour. He had no need to do that. The US would almost certainly not have extended its war on Japan to include Hitler. It would have continued to benefit greatly from providing arms and services to Britain, but would have saved its own efforts for the defeat of the Japs. This time, he was motivated by his antagonism to capitalism, and again, by his hatred of the Jews.

In any case, the Russian war was coming back now to haunt him. This is a point I will take up in my next book. I want now however, to draw attention to how big this Russian war was in the scheme of things. To make the point quickly, I will draw on figures that count the number of persons killed in the entire War, for just a few countries.

British Armed Services deaths were 265,000. American were 170,000. Compared to these, German deaths were 3,250,000 **and Russia lost 13,000,000**.

There is a lot to look at in these and other figures, and for other nations. But the point I am making here is that Russia suffered tremendously. Her heroic efforts in **1942** accounted for about half her total losses, and were much greater that those of any other nation, including Germany. And those same heroic efforts provided the turning point of the War, a point from which the Germans were forced ever backwards.

Joseph Stalin, the leader of the Russians, was never a popular figure with the Western press and governments, and he was often criticised by these, especially when the

War was over. But it is certain that he was just as much behind the Russian success (in the long run) as Churchill and Roosevelt were behind the Allied victories. For me, he was the Man of the Year, and though I have not given him much space in this book, **I am happy to present him, in all his stolidness, on the front cover**.

THE INCREASING ROLE OF WOMEN

Over the course of the year, more and more women were moving from the tradition of home duties into the wide arena of war service. Not everyone thought it wise to do this. Many sensible women argued that their role was to provide stability to their families, most of which now had a man in the military, or were working extraordinary hours in factories, or away building roads with various military bodies.

There were also plenty of others who put their efforts into such bodies as Comforts Funds. These might knit socks for soldiers in the European winters, gather food from anywhere and bundle it up and send it to the Servicemen, or run events to pay for those bundles. For some of the wealthier areas in the cities, this war-time patriotism got mixed into the social whirl, and it was hard to know which was which. But in any event, their efforts were genuine and beneficial.

By the end of the year, though, many women, not all of them young, were occupied in helping in jobs close to the action. Factory workers were producing munitions, ex-architects were driving ambulances, hundreds of girls were picking peas in season, and many were clamouring to get into a proper military Army.

This was all well and good, but it was all very chaotic, and these Letters bemoan below some of the randomness.

Letters, M G. It is exasperating to hundreds of women to read, and hear, daily, of the need of thousands more for war work, when they realise after trying to register that they are "too old" – "45 is the age, madam." I have twice submitted myself for registration for a job, but because I happen to be over the age, although in good physical condition and (without desiring to appear egotistical) capably in many ways, I have to sit back and just listen.

Letters, Unwilling Unemployed War Worker. With reference to the statement by Mr Drakeford that there are still too many fit women in Australia not actively engaged in useful war work I would like to state that I am a very unwilling unemployed war worker. Until a few weeks ago I was doing fabric work in the aircraft repair section of a company working under the Commonwealth Government. Work got slack, and a number of us were put on waiting time. After two weeks of waiting we were told we were no longer needed.

I was very keen on the work, and had had considerable experience. I made inquiries about joining the WAAF as a fabric worker, and was told there were no vacancies. It is not very encouraging after having made the effort to do a war job and run my home as well.

Letters, Gray Chadston. I congratulate Mr E Scott on his most sane and sensible letter. Anybody who would even remotely compare traffic conditions here with those in London even before this war has never been in London. The buses there run slowly only in the city itself, where, instead of regular halts, they stop just at one or two important points; whilst the conductors stand on the step and help passengers to jump on and off the moving vehicle all along the street – far more strenuous work than anything our girls will have to do.

With regard to swift running and swinging fast round corners, you get all that in the London suburbs, and also plenty of narrow and crooked streets. I was in London occasionally during the last war, and I may say that **the girl conductors were most efficient, most resourceful, and most courteous.** They managed the crowds with the greatest ease and good humour, and were given every support and sympathy by both the male personnel and the general public.

Letters, Joyce Nicholls. I wonder if many women in New South Wales feel as disgusted as I feel when reading of the dissatisfaction regarding the salaries for women war workers? It seems to me that women ought to be given twice their usual salaries to take the place of men who have, in some instances under compulsion, had theirs reduced by at least 50 per cent.

Very few women in paid occupations have lost anything by helping the war effort, while the men who, voluntarily or not, are offering their lives to save Australia, are rewarded with **a pittance less than the basic wage**. I say by all means award the workers the full man's salary, but let the major part of it go to supplement the war pay of the soldiers whose jobs they have taken.

Letters, Fair Play. I would like, from a woman's viewpoint, to register a strong protest in regard to the suggested interrogation of people in hotel lounges and other public places. I have given months of service to the Red Cross, have made many camouflage nets, and donate blood regularly to the Sydney Hospital. I don't think I can, therefore, be classed as a "lounge lizard," but if during my infrequent leisure hours I should happen to be having refreshments in a hotel and I am molested by a man-power official, I shall forcibly protest, and I advise every woman to do the same.

It is generally conceded that the country needs the service of every able-bodied woman; very well then – let the Government call us up in a proper manner according to our age and circumstances. As we are all registered it should be relatively simple to classify us. But for the Government to subject women to public inquisition would savour too much of Gestapo methods. It would also be an infringement of personal liberty. We are a British people, living in a democratic community; **let us beware lest the exigencies of the times end in filching from us our cherished liberties.**

Letters, M W. During the last few months there has been a lot said about the Women's Land Army. One is led to believe they are issued with a smart uniform, receive some preliminary training, and then sent to work under good conditions. This is not so.

On applying at the office one finds there is no uniform issued, in fact, one is given a kit list which includes two pairs khaki overalls and blouses, four blankets, towels, bag to use as a hanging wardrobe, plates, and cutlery, all of which one is supposed to buy with one's own coupons and money. This is poor encouragement for any prospective Land Army girl. When she intends to give up her full time and home life to enter one of the Services, she does expect to be issued with her uniform and eating and sleeping requirements.

Letters, E Ogilvie. The employment of girls aged 18-21 to replace young men of the same age, in permanent employment on farms, is not practicable so long as the demand by girls for higher wages than men remains. There is no "farm award." In practice, farm hands have usually been paid somewhat less than "station hand award rates," except for special work or harvesting.

There can, of course, be no comparison between the universal character of the general work, and its economic value, done by a young man of, say, 19, who has lived all his life on a farm, and that of a girl who has scarcely seen a pitchfork or a draught horse. Another serious difficulty has appeared. It has been found that too many girls start with enthusiasm, but become disinterested in their work. They tend to change their employment and try out new work, just at that period in their training by the farmer, when they are beginning to be of some use.

Comment. There was no shortage of organisations that were seeking to pull it all together, including getting women's wages defined by a single body. But such unification was far off. At the end of 1942, and indeed by the end of 1945, such matters had been settled only a little. That is not to detract in any way from the efforts of Oz women during the War. It is simply to say that, if things had been better organized, they would have been even more productive. But then the same is true for the entire War effort. We really could have done better if we had been directed by Hitler. I'm not sure we would have voted for that.

THE GROWTH OF THE RESISTANCE

Since the start of the year, the growth of governmental regulation and interference had grown beyond recognition. This is hardly surprising, given that, in the shortest time imaginable, the nation had to turn from being a gay care-free society into one that was obsessed with its war effort. There was no doubt that everything must change, that people must be conscripted, that freedoms must be curtailed, that priorities must be established.

The conscription for military purposes is the most obvious example of this. **For civilian**s, there was conscription for munitions and other work. All moderate Australians accepted this, and really enjoyed their freedom to grizzle about it. But what gave them a great pain in the neck was when they saw Government ineptitude on a large scale that simply defied any vestige of common sense. Why, they asked, was the Army always harping about a shortage of recruits when so many able bodied men were knocked back at recruiting centres? Why have an age limit of 45 on women for jobs when there was no physical reason for it? Why ban **pink** icing? How many lives or planes would that save?

Why, oh why, did they take our boats away, and then give them back? Why are you now banning the use of housekeepers, when it frees us up to work in munitions? Why now do you say that housekeepers are OK again? Why should advertisements of patent medicines be restricted to 20 words? There were hundreds of such issues, some big and some small, that irritated and confounded ordinary compliant folk. Perhaps, they thought, we should not talk about them. After all, careless talk costs lives. Yet they are silly, and there are so many of them, that surely something can be done. Surely someone with some common sense will take stop the folly.

Well, the good news was that at last there were some signs of sanity returning. From November, the penny dropped in the general population that the Japs would not be invading. From that point onwards, an increasing number of voices could be heard, if you listened hard enough, against the dominance of Government. For example, the Minister for the NES in NSW, Mr Hefron, who was also Premier of the State, became very vocal in his calls for the brown-outs to be completely removed. A meeting of 424 major retailers unanimously voted to reject the call from Mr Dedman to recruit their prime staff (40,000 of them) for the Army.

On top of that, the Letters to the papers took on a different tone. Up till October, they had generally been full of patriotism, all completely in favour of a full war effort, and staunchly advocating austerity. Now they changed so that many more Letters suddenly took a shot at the Government. Are Ministers imposing controls because they have an eye on post-war conditions, and wish now to set up a socialist state? Or perhaps, a totalitarian state? Will our democracy be permanently strangled by the enormous current growth in the numbers of new inspectors and new regulations?

These were timely questions, and were signs that resistance was alive and might start growing. It had a long way to go, and when I tell you that butter and petrol rationing survived till 1950, five years after the War ended, you will appreciate that it had not much immediate success. Still, in my opinion, it was great to see that, in this democracy, there were forces stirring that would continue to press for restraints on self-serving tyrants.

WE SURVIVED OUR TOUGHEST YEAR

1942 was, by my reckoning, Australia's toughest year ever. We started with the unbelievable discovery that the Japs were coming as fast as possible at us, conquering nation after nation and island after island on the way. Over the next six moths or so, they made a bridge-head as close as New Guinea, bombed Darwin at will, and sent subs to shell Sydney and Newcastle.

By July, most Australians were pretty sure that Oz would be invaded and, despite all the defiant talk from our leaders, that we might not be able to hold them back. In the face of this threat, the nation had gone onto a war footing, and produced a lot more than before, consumed a lot less, and worked a lot harder. At the same time, many of our finest men were killed and maimed, far from home, and there were, sadly, many families grieving now, and living in dread of the future. All of this was as bleak as we have ever had it.

But gradually, since Spring, the tide of battles here and in Europe turned, so that by this end of the year, the threat of invasion had gone. And, as some of you might know, the Japanese finally surrendered unconditionally in August, 1945. That was a good thing, but because I have already read my **1943** book, I know that the next two years will be almost as challenging as was 1942.

As I look back at 1942, the one thing that stands out is **the amazing pace of change**. People nowadays, in 2022, say they have trouble keeping up with all the changes that currently beset them. All I can say is **that compared to 1942, they ain't seen nothin' yet**.

Having said that, **I will close up shop now**. The greatest problem I had in writing this book was that I had **to jettison so much material**. I could have written three books. But, despite that, I found it the most enjoyable book to write so far in this series, and **I hope you had as much pleasure in reading as I got from writing.**

COMMENTS FROM READERS

Tom Lynch, Speers Point…..Some history writers make the mistake of trying to boost their authority by including graphs and charts all over the place. You on the other hand get a much better effect by saying things like "he made a pile". Or "every one worked hours longer that they should have, and felt like death warmed up at the end of the shift." I have seen other writers waste two pages of statistics painting the same picture as you did in a few words….

Barry Marr, Adelaide….you know that I am being facetious when I say that I wish the war had gone on for years longer so that you would have written more books about it…

Edna College, Auburn…. A few times I stopped and sobbed as you brought memories of the postman delivering letters, and the dread that ordinary people felt as he neared. How you captured those feelings yet kept your coverage from becoming maudlin or bogged down is a wonder to me….

Betty Kelly. Every time you seem to be getting serious you throw in a phrase or memory that lightens up the mood. In particular, in the war when you were describing the terrible carnage of Russian troops, for no reason, you ended with a ten line description of how aggrieved you felt and ended it with "apart from that, things are pretty good here". For me, it turned the unbearable into the bearable, and I went from feeling morbid and angry back to a normal human being….

Alan Davey, Brisbane….I particularly liked the light-hearted way you described the scenes at the airports as the American high-flying entertainers flew in. I had always seen the crowd behaviour as disgraceful, but your light-hearted description of it made me realise it was in fact harmless and just good fun….

MORE INFORMATION ON THESE BOOKS

Over the past 17 years the author, Ron Williams, has written this series of books that present a social history of Australia in the post-war period. They cover the period for 1939 to 1973, with one book for each year. Thus there are 35 books.

To capture the material for each book, the author, Ron Williams, worked his way through the Sydney Morning Herald and the Age/Argus day-by-day, and picked out the best stories, ideas and trivia. He then wrote them up into 176 pages of a year-book.

He writes in a direct conversational style, he has avoided statistics and charts, and has produced easily-read material that is entertaining, and instructive, and charming.

They are invaluable as gifts for birthdays, Christmas, and anniversaries, and for the oldies who are hard to buy for.

These books are available at all major retailers. They are listed also in all leading catalogues, including Title Page and Dymocks and Booktopia.

Over the nexr few pages, summaries of other books years from 1939 to 1973 in the Series are presented. A synopsis of all books in the Series is available at:

THERE ARE 35 TITLES IN THIS SERIES

For the 35 years from 1939 to 1973

Born in 1939?
What else happened?
Australian Social History

Ron Williams

In 1939, Hitler was the man to watch. He bullied Europe, he took over a few countries, and bamboozled the Brits. By the end of the year, most of Europe ganged up on him, and a phony war had millions of men idling in trenches eating their Christmas turkeys. Back home in Oz, the drunkometer was breathless awaited, pigeon pies were on the nose. Nasho for young men was back, Sinatra led his bobby-soxers, while girls of all ages swooned for crooner Bing.

In 1940, the Brits thought the War would be a picnic. But they changed their mind after military disasters in Norway, Belgium and Tobruk. German subs were filling the Channel with British shipping, and the Frogs stopped hopping. Then the Hun parked their planes full-time over London, and Blitzed it. But, against all odds, the Poms survived. In Oz, the first Menzies Government rationed food, clothing, petrol, smokes and shirt tails. It stopped the use of pink icing on cakes. Photography was suspect, strikes were almost treasonable. Amid all this, Contemporary Art was blossoming, and doing its bit to destroy Australian culture.

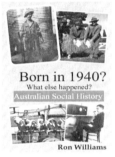

Born in 1940?
What else happened?
Australian Social History

Ron Williams

****

Chrissi and birthday books for Mum and Dad and Aunt and Uncle and cousins and family and friends and work and everyone else.

Don't forget a good read and chuckle for yourself.

In 1943, still went on to introduce butter, clothing, and meat rationing. And he said that domestic service was no longer permissible because of labour shortages. But he relented a bit, and allowed most workers a week's holiday at Christmas. And the blackout covers on all windows could be removed. Though, he added a week later, that they had to go up again. Zoot suits were now for the wearing, fights in city pubs were very popular especially if they involved USA servicemen. But fears of Japanese invasion had gone by year's end.

In 1944, the Japs in the Pacific and the Nazis in Europe were

just about beaten. In Oz, the Labour Government delighted in having great war-time powers, and wanted to extend them. It took a referendum to cool them down. Sydney was invaded by rats, and there were lots of Yankee soldiers in all our cities, and a few of them were not hated. Young girls were being corrupted by the Yanks and by war-time freedom, and clergy were generous with their advice to them. Germany was invaded, but that did not stop the Doodlebugs dropping on London.

AVAILABLE FROM ALL GOOD BOOK STORES AND NEWSAGENTS